GOING DOWN FOR AIR

a memoir in search of a subject

Nearer my God to Thee. Rochester, Kent, England, *circa* 1960.

GOING DOWN FOR AIR

a memoir in search of a subject

Derek Sayer

Paradigm Publishers
Boulder • London

Copyright © 2004 by Paradigm Publishers

Published in the United States by Paradigm Publishers, 3360 Mitchell Lane, Suite C, Boulder, Colorado 80301 USA.

Paradigm Publishers is the trade name of Birkenkamp & Company, LLC, Dean Birkenkamp, President and Publisher.

Library of Congress Cataloging-in-Publication Data has been applied for.

Printed and bound in the United States of America on acid-free paper that meets the standards of the American National Standard for Permanence of Paper for Printed Library Materials.

Designed and Typeset by Straight Creek Bookmakers.

09 08 07 06 05 04 03   5 4 3 2 1

ISBN 1-59451-040-7 (cloth)
ISBN 1-59451-041-5 (paper)

To Yoke-Sum—not forgetting Daniel

Great Barrington Books

Bringing the old and new together
in the spirit of W. E. B. Du Bois

∽ An imprint edited by Charles Lemert ∽

Titles Available

Sociology After the Crisis, Second Edition
by Charles Lemert (2004)

Keeping Good Time: Reflections on Knowledge, Power, and People
by Avery F. Gordon (2004)

Going Down for Air: A Memoir in Search of a Subject
by Derek Sayer (2004)

The Souls of Black Folk
100th Anniversary Edition
by W. E. B. Du Bois, with commentaries by Manning Marable,
Charles Lemert, and Cheryl Townsend Gilkes (2004)

CONTENTS

ACKNOWLEDGMENTS

I AM GRATEFUL FOR THE SUPPORT given to my writing by the Canada Research Chairs program, which I have enjoyed since January 2001. The Canada Foundation for Innovation provided the funding for the Visual Culture Research laboratory at the University of Alberta, where the photographs in this book were edited for publication. Permissions for use of song lyrics and other copyrighted materials are listed separately below.

I entered brief excerpts from what eventually became "A Memoir" in the 2000 Mactaggart Writing Award competition at the University of Alberta. That text formed the basis of a presentation entitled "Anamneses" at the 2000 Congress of the Humanities and Social Sciences, again at the University of Alberta. I much appreciate the encouragement I received from a surprised audience, in particular my colleagues Bill Johnston and Rosalind Sydie. It helped me (in Winston Churchill's immortal words) to keep buggering on. I did not win the writing award, whose prize was $10,000 to be spent on travel in search of new and stimulating experiences (as distinct from academic research)—a wonderful idea. But Mrs. Cécile Mactaggart was sufficiently taken with my entry to offer a "special award," which supported my trip in the fall of 2000 to New Zealand. This book would have been quite different had I not made that journey, halfway across the world and in some ways even further back in time. I am deeply appreciative of Cécile's faith in my writing, and can only hope she thinks the result worthwhile.

I owe thanks to my mother, Mrs. Kathy MacDiarmid, for jogging my memory on this, that, and the other during my time in New Zealand—among many other things—as well as to my brother-in-law Darryl Hughes, who alerted me to articles in *The Wooden Boat* on Maybird, articles that Victor Jackson then triumphantly unearthed for me from the treasure trove that is his study. Doug Aoki, Shyamal Bagchee, Clay Ellis, Karen Engle, Colin Richmond, and Yoke-Sum Wong were all kind enough to read various drafts of "A Memoir." I doubt they will ever know how much their warm responses meant to a writer venturing into uncertain waters, though Yoke-Sum, I suspect, has an inkling. Dariusz Gafijczuk, Lilia Verchinina, and Joshua Nichols all read "In Search of a Subject," and offered the informed and incisive suggestions one expects of good graduate students. Some of these suggestions were gladly taken up. Departing from conventional genres of academic writing, I soon discovered, can rapidly leave one short of publishers. I am correspondingly grateful to Charles Lemert and Dean Birkenkamp at Paradigm for their support of this book, as well as to Christine Arden for her expert and sensitive copy-editing.

"A Memoir" is full of people who long ago took up residence in my memory—family, friends, teachers, colleagues. Some are now dead, others I have lost touch with over the years. What they have meant to me should be plain from the text. But I did not ask their permission to put them in my book. It is all the more important, then, to emphasize that I portray them in these pages not as they are—or even, perhaps, as they were. They appear here as I remember them. And as I hope this book shows, memory is not to be trusted.

LIST OF PHOTOGRAPHS

PRELUDE: WALTER BENJAMIN'S CABINET

⊸

> I put down the cup and turn to my mind. It is up to my mind to find the truth. But how? What grave uncertainty, whenever the mind seems overtaken by itself; when it, the seeker, is also the obscure country where it must seek and where all its baggage will be nothing to it.
>
> —Marcel Proust, *In Search of Lost Time*[1]

THE BEST-KNOWN EPISODE in Marcel Proust's *In Search of Lost Time* is that moment in which the narrator suddenly finds the little town of Combray, where he spent his childhood, flooding back, the memory unexpectedly released by the taste of a *petite madeleine* dipped in tea. Proust compares this process of "involuntary memory" to "that game in which the Japanese amuse themselves by filling a porcelain bowl with water and steeping in it little pieces of paper until then indistinct, which, the moment they are immersed in it, stretch and shape themselves, colour and differentiate, become flowers, houses, human figures, firm and recognizable. . . ."[2] A less benign, though no less involuntary, image of recovered memory is offered by Walter Benjamin in his essay "One-Way Street." "We have long forgotten," he says, "the ritual by which the house of our life was erected. But when it is under assault and enemy bombs are already taking their toll, what enervated, perverse antiquities do they not lay bare in the foundations! What things were interred and sacrificed amid magic incantations, what horrible cabinet of curiosities lies there below, where the deepest shafts are reserved for what is most commonplace?"[3]

For reasons I do not pretend to understand—the slow advance of age, perhaps, or maybe upheavals in my personal life at the time—many things I thought I had long forgotten, or to which, at least, I had formerly attached little importance, started to come back to me around the turn of my fiftieth year. The experience was more Benjaminian than Proustian. There was never as dramatic or complete a single moment of recollection as Proust's sudden rediscovery of the Combray he had thought was completely dead to him. It was a matter, rather, of a subtle shift in the tenor of the present, in which the familiar, everyday things surrounding me—a picture in a book, a tune on the radio—took on added layers of significance, pointing somewhere other than their here and now, back into the recesses of my past. I found myself increasingly drawn *there below*, into the freshly exposed foundations. I could not resist opening Benjamin's cabinet of curiosities. It did not horrify me, though there were some oddities that might well appall others stashed away in its drawers. But I was often surprised, to say the least, by what I found there. The more drawers I unlocked, the curiouser and curiouser their contents became. Each resembled nothing so much as one of those enigmatic but strangely haunting boxes the artist Joseph Cornell manufactured in his basement on Utopia Parkway in Queens, New York; a miniature world, evidently filled with meaning, but a meaning that was impossible, somehow, to pin down.

In one drawer, quite early in my rummagings, I found a toilet with a worn wooden seat and a chain I couldn't quite reach, an unaccountably unpleasant box of buttons, BBC radio broadcasts of cricket Test Matches between England and Australia, a biscuit barrel, the twinkling red and green lights of planes landing at night at London Airport, the name of a lodger, and the beige smell of Brasso. In another I discovered the warmth of a paraffin heater, Players Weights, George Orwell's *A Clergyman's Daughter* taking a bath she never did in the book, a Christmas carol, a Texan friend comparing sucking on a barbecued duck leg to the pleasures of cunnilingus, a Venus with a beautiful backside, and the coldness of the playing fields above the River Medway where I used to play hockey from January to March. A third drawer contained my first kiss and a mousy architect leaving his flamboyant wife for his secretary, sandwiched between Tuscany and Bohemia. A fourth was opened by a book of erotic photographs I stumbled across in a bookstore behind the La Scala opera house in Milan, mostly devoted to flagellation, which might as well have been labeled "Drink Me." A veritable cornucopia, this one; its contents included a record of Lotte Lehmann singing Schumann's *Lieder*, W. G. Sebald's *The Rings of Saturn*, a postcard sent to my mother from The Hague, a *Wienerschnitzel alla milanese*, my right hand repeatedly reaching down for a gear-stick that wasn't there in New Zealand, a performance of Verdi's *Nabucco* in a Czech coal and steel town up near the Polish border, and a paper-knife hammered out of shrapnel by my great-grandfather Pa during the Battle of the Somme.

Though, in a manner of speaking, one thing always led to another, there was little apparent logic to the cabinet's ordering. Things were jumbled together with no concern for provenance, propinquity, or chronology. Recent travel journals were placed side by side with toys from my earliest childhood. A red-faced stevedore singing "The Sash My Father Wore" in the Medway Folk Club near Rochester Bridge was mixed up with Pete Seeger singing for Nicaragua in a church in Manhattan, teenage girls whose bodies I had once touched, the tubes coming out of my dying grandmother's nose, and a moth-eaten donkey jacket that belonged to my father. The contents of the various drawers were certainly not ordered according to the tidy times and spaces of an autobiography. The carelessness in the transcriptions of the fragments of poetry, snatches of popular song, and incidents from novels, which littered the collection, was no less disconcerting, particularly given my usual scholarly fastidiousness with regard to matters of referencing. Yet this seeming shambles was plainly not the result of neglect, for if ever I opened a drawer for a second look, I would find that its contents had been carefully rearranged while I was away. By whom, I was never quite sure.

If the collection's logic escaped me, I nevertheless found an uncanny coherence in the bits and pieces that had been gathered together in one or another drawer, though I would be hard put to say in what, exactly, this coherence consisted. The objects in the cabinet had obviously been chosen with care (though not, in any conscious manner, by me), and their placement, while not always comprehensible, was anything but haphazard. In the manner of surrealist painting and poetry, the juxtaposition of otherwise unrelated items often seemed oddly fitting, and was sometimes unexpectedly affecting—though, once again, I could seldom put my finger on quite why these coincidences should have moved me as they did. The more drawers I opened, the more I discovered, too, that certain items turned up again and again. These recurrences gave a consistency to the collection—almost as if, could we but decode their significance, they might provide its keys. Among them were open, flat landscapes, big empty skies, tobacco smoke, garbled passages from *The Lord of the Rings*, mementoes of the British Empire, and friends who died young. In drawer after drawer I found rattan canes, of the kind once used on small boys' bottoms in English public schools. I was not wholly unaware of the attraction such implements had long held for me, though I never could fathom it. It was one of those things I had thrust to the back of my mind. But the extent of the fascination these objects evidently exerted over whoever had been responsible for assembling the cabinet came as a shock. He had seemingly hunted down and hoarded anything and everything that whispered in his ear the childish word *spanking*.

Perhaps the most curious feature of the cabinet struck me only later, after I had largely ceased what were at one time my almost nightly visits. It was what was not there. Though I had sifted through its drawers many times, I found, for instance, no graduation photographs, laudatory reviews of my books, or other souvenirs of an academic life, beyond the occasional gnostic quotation from Wittgenstein or Derrida. The few junctures where the contents of the cabinet touched on this domain to which I had devoted my adult years at first seemed random. I subsequently realized that they almost always recalled trivial encounters, brushed aside at the time—encounters in which, for whatever reason, that academic life had momentarily lost its sense: the theme of "Colonel Bogey" being picked up by a sitarist from a car-horn in Delhi, a feeling of ridiculousness during a conversation at a dinner party in Glasgow, an embarrassment in a pub in Durham, filed in the same drawer as a choked treble solo in Rochester Cathedral. There were other, no less puzzling gaps in the collection, which I need not go into here.

Suffice it to say that I had no difficulty at all in recognizing that the contents of the cabinet—including, I am sorry to say, the *frisson* occasioned by the solidity of the Victorian hairbrushes and the flexibility of the schoolroom canes—were beyond a shadow of a doubt the detritus of *my* life. All the same, this curious assortment of bric-a-brac did not correspond, in either its presences or its absences, to that life as *I* would normally have related it. It was not the confection of what Proust calls my "voluntary memory, the memory of the intelligence,"[4] the work of the self I am accustomed to recognizing in the mirror.

4

This gap is the space within which *Going Down for Air* is situated, not just as a personal anamnesis, though it is that, but also as the site of a wider inquiry into what social theorists have taken to calling *the subject*.

THIS BOOK, WHOSE TITLE vulgarly plays on George Orwell's novel of a middle-aged man revisiting the haunts of his childhood and coming up disappointed, is unlike any I have written before, or might have expected myself to write. Its origin, as I have said, was fortuitous. Growing out of my rummagings in Walter Benjamin's cabinet, it is first and foremost an exploration of the workings of memory itself—of what we remember, how we remember, and how much, in the course of remembering, we forget; of the tricks memory plays, mutating times and places, cutting here, pasting there, reconciling presents and pasts in pictures as firm and recognizable as that of Proust's Combray—pictures so true to life they can sometimes convince us that we remember things we never experienced at all. Lacking access to anybody else's memory, I have trawled my own. I doubt it operates much differently than other people's. This does not pretend, however, to be a scientific study, and one does not have to be an academic to read it. I would far rather it provided the voyeuristic pleasure that any good biographical writing should, which comes from intruding on somebody else's privacy, and discovering, maybe, something of oneself lurking behind the curtains.

But since I remain a sociologist, as well as a man turning fifty, my professional interest was also piqued by what I found in Benjamin's cabinet. So this book is a study, too, of how every memory, no matter how intimate or personal it may be, entrammels us in a symbolic order that everywhere surpasses us, and endlessly recuperates our sociality, sewing us into universes of meaning that are greater than ourselves. Sometimes this can happen in the most perverse of ways—those rattan canes, for instance, returning as the fetishistic objects of an inexplicable, but quite unmistakably *English,* adult desire. Not for nothing is flagellation known as *la vice anglaise:* the cane was the symbolic *point de capiton* of the English public school I attended from eight to seventeen, which was in its turn an imagined microcosm of the playing fields of Empire. I cannot escape muscular Christianity and the White Man's Burden, even in—and perhaps especially in, since my rational self rejects such untimely nostalgias—the solitary intimacies of sexual fantasy. Why should we expect the bonds that link self and Other in what we too glibly call "society" to be conscious, rational, or decent? Nowhere do we turn out to be more enduringly social, in fact, than in the most private and murky closets of our minds. For this reason, I believe the study of memory, in all its irrationality, belongs at the very heart of sociology.

The first text in *Going Down for Air,* which I have simply called "A Memoir," is just that—my own recollections, mostly of a childhood and adolescence spent in the southeast corner of England, the Atlantic Ocean and half a lifetime away, lit with the usual puzzlements and nostalgias. Like any memoir, mine calls up times and places forever gone, filtered through the lens of the here and now in which I am writing. Somewhere in there, sliding between the one and the other, is a subjectivity—a very English, imperial, public school subjectivity, queerly masculine, caught on the cusp of the extinction of the world in and of which it made sense. Unlike an autobiography, however, this memoir does not try to tell a coherent story, to force recollection into the mold of a narrative of a life. Over the course of eighteen months, when the mood took me, I sat down and recorded my memories as they came, in the flow of words that first came to mind. The result was a text linked together by associations and evocations rather than by chronology, logic, or plot, shuttling back and forth between present and past. But this, after all, is *how memory works.* And from the point of view of a sociologist, what this text *shows* about how memory works is perhaps the most interesting thing about it.

When I came to edit the text for publication, I did nothing that would have imposed an extraneous order or sense on the words I had written, after the fact. I limited myself to providing a separate set of notes that explained allusions to books, songs, radio programs, events, and so on that might otherwise have been obscure. Nor did I censor out what might, for some, be disturbing passages, evidence of what a friend who read the manuscript delicately described as "the young narrator's ambiguous homoerotic sensibility." It was important, as far as possible, to retain *the words that first came to mind* because of the traces they carry with them, recalling other times, other places, and other users of the same words. Our own words are never our words *alone.* They are witnesses to a socialization whose complication, most of the time, we scarcely even begin to guess at. In my case, the categorical grids sociologists all too often impose on the world in the guise of making sense of it, whether they be the overly neat dichotomies of colonizer and colonized, the pieties of race/class/gender, or the bipolar simplifications of sexual identity and orientation, soon unravelled once I crossed the borders of Proust's obscure country. I suspect the same would be true for anyone else. Sociologists might venture into this terrain more often, if only to ponder how this wild profusion of gambolling signifiers is marshalled, despite all odds, into the identities we all too readily take for granted.

The second text in the book, which I have called "In Search of a Subject," addresses the connection between memory and identity less idiosyncratically—though I am not sure that means any more cogently. There are costs, as well as benefits, to the perennial academic search for clarity. Written a year or so later, this essay is a more theoretical reflection on how memory works to sustain identity, both individual and social. In its form, at least, it is a more conventional intellectual exercise. It does not violate the rules of grammar, stretch the bounds of sense, or interrupt the narrative with garbled fragments of poetry, pornographic fantasies that won't politely go away, or lines of half-remembered pop songs. It makes its case through the familiar academic media of textual criticism and reasoned argument. Drawing on a range of semiotic and psychoanalytic thinkers (Lacan, Derrida, Barthes), as well as on photographic images and literary texts (Baudelaire, Kundera, Breton), it suggests that identity is something that can be achieved only in the realm of the imaginary, in an *imago* of the self which is (mis)taken for the subject, leaving behind a trail of unassimilated detritus that returns in the subversions of the unconscious. This is in itself by no means an original argument. Where my essay may perhaps further discussion is in its contention that it is in memory, above all, that this *imago* attains its solidity—and that memory may equally undo that composure. For the concreteness of this *imago* is not anchored, as we like to believe, in a real past that is encapsulated in our memories. Memory is able to undergird our social personae to the extent that it is itself, as Milan Kundera once put it, a form of forgetting. The solidity of the *imago* is the effect of language's ability to create verisimilitude in an eternal present of signification—and its unity remains correspondingly precarious, because language is a slippery and treacherous thing, ever ready to spirit us away.

Family snapshots aside, the photographs in this book are my own, taken during the time I was writing it. None of them have been digitally altered. They are not montages, though many involve reflections. What I photographed was what I saw, and what I saw was what I chanced upon. Rather than attempt some elaborate theoretical justification for the inclusion of what are plainly not straightforward illustrations, which might take me into Benjamin's discussion of the optical unconscious and André Breton's ruminations on the found object,[5] let me say simply that these pictures seemed to belong—they were another way of navigating the same quotidian, yet sometimes strikingly unsettling landscape this book endeavors to explore. One chooses what to photograph, certainly—but within the limits of what fortuitously engages the eye, and often without altogether knowing why. Not unlike writing—much as we might prefer to believe that a text is nothing more than a reflection of its author's conscious intentions, words whose meaning he can authoritatively pin down in an introduction that tells readers what they can expect to find in his work.[6]

Derek Sayer

Edmonton, December 8, 2003

NOTES

1. Marcel Proust, *The Way by Swann's*, Volume 1 of *In Search of Lost Time*, translated by Lydia Lewis, London: Penguin/Allen Lane, 2002, p. 48.

2. *Ibid.*, p. 50.

3. Walter Benjamin, "One-Way Street," in *Selected Writings: Volume 1, 1913–1926*, edited by Marcus Bullock and Michael W. Jennings, Cambridge, Mass.: The Belknap Press of Harvard University Press, 1996, p. 445.

4. Proust, *The Way by Swann's*, p. 46.

5. See *inter alia* Walter Benjamin, "Little History of Photography," in *Selected Writings: Volume 2, 1927–1934*, edited by Michael W. Jennings, Howard Eiland, and Gary Smith, Cambridge, Mass.: The Belknap Press of Harvard University Press, pp. 507–530; Rosalind E. Krauss, *The Optical Unconscious*, Cambridge, Mass.: MIT Press, 1993; and André Breton, *Mad Love*, Lincoln: University of Nebraska Press, 1987, pp. 25–38.

6. See further Roland Barthes, "The Death of the Author," in *Image, Music, Text*, New York: Hill and Wang, 1977.

A MEMOIR

⟶

Time present and time past
Are both perhaps present in time future,
And time future contained in time past.
If all time is eternally present
All time is unredeemable.
What might have been is an abstraction
Remaining a perpetual possibility
Only in a world of speculation.
What might have been and what has been
Point to one end, which is always present.
Footfalls echo in the memory
Down the passage which we did not take
Towards the door we never opened
Into the rose-garden. My words echo
Thus, in your mind.

     —T. S. Eliot, "Burnt Norton," from *The Four Quartets*

CECI N'EST-PAS UNE PIPE, reads the legend under the pipe in René Magritte's picture. This here is not a pipe.

Nasi goreng, potato croquettes from automats, French fries—chips, I would have called them then—eaten out of paper cones with mayonnaise as the mists curled in off the North Sea. Above all, the sweet hovering fragrance, sweet as a confectionery store, of Dutch pipe tobacco.

It was a place where Jean-Paul Belmondo roomed with the Penguin Modern European Poets, a time when you were never alone with a Strand. The mists were already familiar to me from Albert Camus' The Fall which I read at sixteen, around the time I first encountered surrealist art. The fog on the Zuyderzee, muzzling against the windowpanes, conjured up a landscape of teenage longings. *Female smells in shuttered rooms / and cigarettes in corridors / and cocktail smells in bars.* Gordon Comstock futilely raging in George Orwell's Keep the Aspidistra Flying. The spy in The Ipcress File, who smoked Gauloises blues and didn't have a name. Chet Baker would have been there too, only he hadn't fallen out of that Amsterdam hotel window yet, thinking he could fly. The manner of his death, two decades later, confirms all I remember about the Low Countries.

Just possibly that is why I still smoke today—out of nostalgia.

Other tobaccos, other smells, recall other, older selves. Older, because more distant in time: a paradox, nicely caught in what was most profoundly disturbing in Dennis Potter's Blue Remembered Hills, the adult actors dressed in children's clothes. Bondman's Number One, I think it was called, thick wads of acrid black tobacco wrapped in crinkly waxed paper in round one-ounce tins. The rack of stubby briars that Pa, my mother's grandfather, kept on the mantel shelf. The chipped mug of Oxo Pa took with fingers of dry toast and a sprinkle of white pepper at eleven o'clock every morning. A twice-weekly journey with my mother on the Central Line of the London Underground, which ceased when I was five: White City, East Acton, North Acton, Hanger Lane, Perivale, Greenford.

Bapaume—carved on a paper knife Pa hammered out of shrapnel for his only daughter Ivy, my mother's mother.

Mustard gas wafting over Flanders fields, crossing the Channel to rub its yellow back against my windowpanes. The miserable sprout from Brussels, as Elizabeth David once called it, which Pa showed me proudly growing in his garden.

A solitary blasted tree menacing against the night sky.

His memories, mine.

I WISH TO EXPLORE—lose myself in, divert around, linger over, rummage through, savor—these thickets of memory. What then, if anything, ties *my* five-year-old self listening to World War I reminiscences in Pa's Greenford garden to my seventeen-year-old *self* on his first solo trip abroad by cross-Channel ferry to Ostend and Amsterdam, imagining he is Jack Kerouac? What links either of these recollected selves to the almost fifty-year-old man writing this who smokes Camels and lives in Edmonton, Alberta, Canada—other than the contingent connectivity of tobacco smells and things that waft: mists and mustard gas—the entire train of thought

originating in nothing more than looking once more, and for no particular reason, at René Magritte's painting The Treachery of Images?

Would it be the same me I am remembering had some other chance
encounter (say, with Vera Lynn singing We'll Gather Lilacs in the Spring
Again) sent my mind spinning off down some other Memory Lane? Why,
anyway, is that song—like the same composer's Keep the Home Fires
Burning—guaranteed to bring tears to my eyes, no matter how many
times I hear it, no matter, too, that I did not personally experience either
of the World Wars these songs so poignantly, so exactly recall?

> *You might hear laughin', spinnin',*
> *swingin' madly across the sun,*
> *it's not aimed at anyone,*
> *it's just escapin' on the run,*
> *and but for the sky there are no fences facin'.*

See? Bob Dylan, Hey Mister Tambourine Man; me, *circa* 1965. Bringing
it all back home. I quote from memory, a memory jogged in this instance
by my own use of the word *spinning*. I loved that song. Transfixed by the
beauty of its poetry, the fleet-footedness of its images, I had no desire to
pin down its meaning in prose. Still, the words seem apt here:

> *Take me disappearin'*
> *through the smoke rings of my mind,*
> *down the foggy ruins of time,*
> *far past the frozen leaves,*
> *the haunted, frightened trees,*
> *out to the windy beach,*
> *far from the twisted reach of crazy sorrow.*

Smokes, fogs, trees, seas—things randomly connected, freely associat-
ed, just escaping on the run. Yet oh so coherent, making a consummate
sense that lies beyond the bounds of logic, or, maybe, of that which is
capable of being stated at all. Or so it feels.

Wittgenstein: *There are, indeed, things that cannot be put into words.*
They **make themselves manifest**.

Is there a statute of limitations on possible memories and the infinite
selves they engender, kaleidoscoping the spinning fragments into ever-

new patterns? Where might recollections of the Indian railways (smoke, spices, sweat, shit, sweet scalding tea drunk from the little red clay pots whose shards littered the tracks), the scent of cloves drying in the sun on the sidewalks in Zanzibar, have taken me already—these memories that are equally and unquestionably mine?

Trying to capture this ceaseless flux, Marcel Proust shut himself up for years in a cork-lined room, going out only to sample the night. What set him off was the remembered taste of a cookie.

BOMBAY AIRPORT, DECEMBER 1969. A dark high-ceilinged restaurant with familiar menus, kormas and vindaloos as English as fish and chips, the waiters in costumes straight out of Carry On Up the Khyber. The same burgundy flock wallpaper you find on curry-house walls in Birmingham or Bradford or Camden Town. The same grimy colonnades at the railway station, appropriately named Victoria Terminus. The same clerks ranged behind their ticket wickets, just as solidly Victorian. I am politely prevented from buying a third-class ticket to Delhi, a two-day trip. I wind up traveling first class, in sole possession of an air-conditioned carriage.

It will take me some time to realize what is already clear in these gestures—that I have my place in this world, and it is not mine to choose. Just another young puppy getting his first taste of the colonies, wet behind the ears, repeating an old journey.

What should they know of England, who only England know?

Sitting on the steps with the train door open I take in villages, fields, buffaloes, brown-skinned women working the earth with hoes. My heart swells up in my throat like some gigantic balloon. I say to myself: *This is my place. These are my people.* I wave. It is embarrassing to recall it. But I do, and rather more sharply than if it were just yesterday.

Before long I shall take a servant.

At some time during those first weeks it hits me that nothing in my head has remotely equipped me to deal with the realities I am encountering. Least of all anything I have learned in my first year at university. My concepts are irrelevant, my images awry. Words lose their grip. The quartertones in an old woman's voice, quavering to a harmonium in a language I don't understand, move me inexpressibly. A sitarist picks up the refrain of Colonel Bogey from a car horn in the street outside, weaves it into his raga, and my world—First World, Second World, Third World—unravels.

I don't try to put Humpty together again, then or later. But there is the usual flotsam: most affectingly, I don't know why, the liquid, loping lines of George Harrison's While My Guitar Gently Weeps playing on a juke-box between tunes from Hindi movies in a Delhi tea-house. Sometimes, when I hear that song, I have exactly Proust's sense of time irretrievably lost—an apprehension of nothing definable, except that it might have been and wasn't—a flickering regret for a passing moment when I was open to the otherness of the world, high on my own insignificance in the great scheme of things, suspending all judgment.

Like a rolling stone. How did it feel? Exhilarating.

I know—I knew soon enough—that it cannot be. I came back to England, finished my degree, learned to trade in the glittering specie of theory.

Footfalls echo in the memory
Down the passage which we did not take
Towards the door we never opened
Into the rose garden.
Go, go, go, said the bird: human kind
Cannot bear very much reality.

Years later, channel surfing, I light for ten minutes or so on a PBS documentary. The professor, a distinguished Afro-American advocate for social causes, leans out of the window of a slow train in Tanzania where he is traveling in search of identity. I feel sorry for him. Where everyone's skin is black, being black signifies nothing. It is the difference of being American that defines him, here.

He is waving like children do from school buses, at distant strangers working in the fields.

THE CANVAS IN THE WINDOW in another Magritte canvas, on which is painted a picture of the view it obscures. The painting is called La Condition Humaine. How do we *know* that behind the picture is what the picture depicts? So much of our life is passed in halls of mirrors.

It was not an epiphanous moment, more a nagging away at the back of my mind. One of those gray Scottish days made up of equal parts mist and drizzle when earth and sky cannot be told apart. Sometime in the early 1980s, likely in summer since we had hoped to conclude the outing with some blackberry picking. We drove, endlessly down it seemed, winding between the knots of the hills. I remember thinking how far it was from the nearest town—how isolated. It would have been a tidy journey two centuries ago on foot or by horse and cart. The object of our visit was New Lanark, a model industrial village founded by David Dale in 1785 and purchased by his son-in-law Robert Owen in 1799.

Whether by then I still considered myself a socialist I don't remember. I am not even sure whether I would have known at the time. To be *on the left* had long since become the glue of old friendships, the currency of dinner party conversation, rather than something requiring belief—or its examination. Certainly whatever passions of justice had animated me in my late teens and twenties were spent. If that is what they ever were. I suspect an older compound.

First equal. Another truly excellent term, says Dr. Gilbert the chemistry master on my school report for the Lent Term of 1964, when I was thirteen years and four months old. In English, normally my best subject, the master's comment is *Disgraceful,* the position thirtieth, next to bottom in the class. *He must learn to apply himself to work which does not interest him.* My form master observes that *He can be very irritating at times,* warning of the harm I can do with my *bitter tongue and pugnacious behavior.* The Head Master sighs *He is obviously able; but he has yet to learn the responsibility this places upon him not only to do the best with his gifts, but also to use them in serving rather than outwitting others.* Many times in subsequent years that sharp and kindly canon of the Church of England saved my bacon, including in the first term of the Upper Sixth when he suspended me from school until the A Level Examinations, which I would be allowed to sit, he wrote my parents, as long as I showed up *in school uniform, clean-shaven, and with hair of a respectable length.*

Need I add anything?

One thing, maybe. The year I got that report I kept a hard-cover notebook, entirely additional to my schoolwork, into which I neatly copied the structures of organic chemistry molecules, a design for a gasworks that could be built in a school laboratory (Dr. Gilbert allowed me to build it for the Prize Day exhibition that summer), and other Chemistry trivia. The item that took me longest to copy out—measuring, ruling, coloring—was the Periodic Table of the Elements. Its symmetries entranced me, the familial groups down, the ascending series across, the spaces already there for as yet undiscovered elements to be slotted into place.

From Mendeleev to Marx is not such a long journey. I still have the notebooks from my PhD, long passages copied out from the Grundrisse and Capital, sentences underlined with wax crayons in a color code to which I have long since forgotten the key. *A thing of beauty is a joy forever,* says Keats—and ideas can be the most blindingly beautiful things of all.

I was introduced to John Keats not by Taffy Williams the English master but by Brian Gilbert, a pretty boy on whom I had a passing crush around the time I was excelling at Chemistry. An odd coincidence of Gilberts, neither of whom somehow fitted—not Brian's effeminate gushing, nor the chemistry master's yellow bow tie. Both left the school the next year.

> *Heard melodies are sweet, but those unheard*
> *Are sweeter; therefore, ye soft pipes, play on;*
> *Not to the sensual ear, but, more endear'd,*
> *Pipe to the spirit ditties of no tone.*

Whether or not I was still a believer, Robert Owen remained a part of the furniture of my mind, inhabiting the same sentimental lumber-rooms as the siege of Leningrad, La Passionara declaring *No pasaran!* and the working-class heroes of the Red Clyde. It was not quite a pilgrimage, but I came to New Lanark expecting to pay my respects. I don't know what else I expected. It says something about me then, I think, that I had no physical image of the place in my mind.

What I found repelled me. It reminded me more than anything else of an army barracks. The streets laid out in straight rows on the hillside. The low, mean, uniform sandstone tenements where the workers were housed. The four mills, towering at five stories, so palpably the center of the enterprise. The grandiloquently titled Institute for the Formation of Character, where Owen personally gave the little boys military drill and the little girls lessons in dancing and deportment—a bleak environmentalist pedagogy as imprisoning of the future as the graceless architecture.

Ceci n'est-pas. Siena, Italy, 2001.

Innocence petrified while time passed it on by—just like the young lovers on Keats's Grecian urn, only a good deal uglier. As I walked around the colony, a phrase from The Communist Manifesto kept hammering at the doors of my mind.

The inexhaustible productive powers of modern industry.

The sudden shock of the old, when encountered on its own terms—not as we have remembered it.

JUST HOW FAR BACK DOES IT GO, this self that can be derailed by such chance encounters, only to be put back on track again, and again, and again—a very long division with remainder? What is it Walter Benjamin says?

We have long forgotten the ritual by which the house of our life was erected. But when it is under assault and enemy bombs are already taking their toll, what enervated, perverse antiquities do they not lay bare in the foundations! What things were interred and sacrificed amid magic incantations, what horrible cabinet of curiosities lies there below, where the deepest shafts are reserved for what is most commonplace?

Nanny and Grandad, my maternal grandmother and grandfather, lived next door to Nana and Pa their entire married lives until Grandad went to New Zealand after Nanny died when I was twelve or maybe just thirteen. Their house on Hill Rise in Greenford on the western fringes of London is a scattering of sharply focused remembrances, metonyms that stand for but never quite add up to a whole. The white porcelain toilet with the worn wooden seat and the hanging chain I couldn't reach. The bone-handled table knife, sharpened down the years to a third of its original size, that Nanny always used for chopping parsley. The stench of the rabbit I once watched her gut, its intestines steaming in a bucket on the back steps. Her fat thighs wobbling as she fastened her suspenders, one leg up on the bed.

Pinky-gray powder puffs on perspiring white flesh.

A box of buttons, big and small, ornate and plain, wood and cloth, brass and bone, tipped out on the eiderdown, harmless objects to which I took a wholly unreasonable dislike. I still find Bob Hope's signature tune Buttons and Bows vaguely sinister, and not just because with every face-lift the man comes more and more to recall Dorian Grey—a deceitful warp, somehow, in the moral fabric of time.

One day nearly half a century later she tells me she used to collect buttons, all kinds of buttons, as a child. The old memory flits across my mind, and I am suddenly uneasy—as if this were a bad omen. I fear the shadow of the past, the boy tripping up the man.

BBC Radio broadcasts of the Oxford and Cambridge Boat Race, Test Matches between England and Australia. Middlesex, a large and mysterious book with three long lions engraved in gold leaf on the red cloth binding of the cover, over which I spent hours poring. The dented brass biscuit barrel, its contents sparingly dispensed with tea. Custard creams, ginger snaps, pink wafers, bourbons, which Nanny bought loose from the serried ranks of square glass-topped tins at Woolworth on Greenford Broadway. I still remember the name of the lodger, John Brunston, the slow twinkling red and green lights of the planes coming down at night over London Airport.

Newspapers were laid out on the table, rags (one for cleaning, one for polishing) and fingers turned inexorably black. The milky beige smell of Brasso lingered on the hands long after the keepsakes had been burnished and put back in their places till they were ready to be taken out and handled once more. A Spanish galleon in full sail across a serving-platter, Pa's copper-bound shell cases from Bapaume or Wipers or Verdun.

I was four—five at most. It must have been on a weekend because we drove down to Greenford from the flat in Kilburn in the black Austin Seven instead of going by tube. I had been playing in the rightaway behind the house where I got into an altercation with another boy. I boasted that I threw sand in his face—which I hadn't. It was a handful of ivy, ripped off a wall. Dad demanded I say sorry. I refused. *He called me names!* Dad promptly turned me upside down over his knee. Trying to impress Grandad, I suppose. My bottom throbbed in the back of the car all the way home.

I was sent to bed without any dinner, in the room where the mustard gas rubbed its back against the windowpanes. The yellow seeped in from the sodium lamp outside. Often, in that room, I was frightened by car headlights scanning the ceiling.

Later that night my mother brought me my dinner on a wooden tray upon which she had carefully arranged all my toy dogs.

A MOTIF, A REFRAIN, ECHOING DOWN THE YEARS, shifting its shape with the times. One of those tunes you can't get out of your head no matter how hard you try.

My cabinet of curiosities contains some undoubted perversities, salted away from prying eyes when my years were still numbered in single digits. An illustration in one of my father's few books of a guard in a Japanese prisoner-of-war camp flicking away with a bamboo cane at the naked buttocks of a British officer, first the right and then the left, until—I have not forgotten the description—they were *a mass of bloody weals*. What impressed me most was that all the while the soldier continued to squat stoically, weaving baskets. I was equally captivated by a drawing in our Latin primer of a boy supported on the shoulders of four of his fellows as his tutor flogged his bare backside with a bundle of ferulae. Our form master, the hearty, popular, and occasionally apoplectic

Mr. Trett, told us how they did things properly in those days. Small boys like us were whipped, naked, in the marketplace in Sparta to make them into men.

Punishment will come whenever I desire to give it. You need not be disobedient to merit it. I will punish when it pleases me. Sometimes that will be the only reason for it.

The sufferings of Job. Nearer my God to Thee.

Thirty odd years later, sipping an ouzo in the empty square with the orange trees, I remembered them—the Spartan boys, I mean. A sleepy town in the Peloponnese, with precious few ruins to show for all that ancient bravado. *Remember the baths by which you were slain* warns the epigraph to the third poem in George Seferis's Mythical Story:

> *I awoke with this marble head in my hands*
> *which exhausts my elbows and I do not know where to set it*
> *down.*
> *It was falling into the dream as I was coming out of the dream*
> *so our lives joined and it will be very difficult to part them.*
> *I look at the eyes: neither open nor closed*
> *I speak to the mouth which keeps trying to speak*
> *I hold the cheeks which have passed beyond the skin.*
> *I have no more strength.*
> *My hands disappear and come back to me*
> *mutilated.*

Seferis belongs with Prévert and Apollinaire among the Penguin Modern European Poets alongside Kerouac and Eliot and the other denizens of Amsterdam's mists. I stole this particular volume, Four Greek Poets, from the SPCK Bookstore in the church beside Rochester Cathedral when I was sixteen. The slim Penguins slipped easily into the inside pocket of my school blazer. I no more knew what Mythical Story was about then than I did Bob Dylan's Visions of Johanna or Desolation Row—and nor, for the same reasons, did I care. A couple of years later, as an undergraduate at Essex University, I persuaded myself it was an allegory of modern alienation.

Seferis's cycle speaks to me now of the poignancy of recollection, which is undoubtedly both mythic and storied; of the necessity and impossibility of connecting presents with pasts; of the burdens of memories that are ours—yet not.

> *Having known this fate of ours so well*
> *wandering around among broken stones, three or six thousand*
> *years*
> *searching in collapsed buildings which might have been our*
> *homes*
> *trying to remember dates and heroic deeds:*
> *shall we now be able?*

A bus ride above Sparta lies Mystras, a once prospering Byzantine town of maybe forty thousand people, vacant today save for a few Orthodox nuns and monks, reminders of just how far east this cradle of western civilization has traveled in the millennia that have slipped by since they whipped small boys in the marketplace. Doe-eyed Christian saints keep watch in the silent churches. Greece is an affront to narrative proprieties, Myceneans and Macedonians, Byzantines and Franks, Venetians and Ottomans all indecently layered in a riot of ancient miscegenations. Pausanias may still serve as a reliable guide as you hear the pipes of Homer's shepherd on the dry slopes above Mycenae, walk the broad-paved streets of Old Corinth in the footsteps of Saint Paul—or not.

One Wednesday afternoon when we were lining up for games another pupil, Kevin or Michael or Richard Phair was his name, slipped down his gym shorts in the playground to show off the souvenirs of the caning he had received the night before. A slight fair-haired kid, not the sort to get into trouble. The neat red stripes were already turning purply-blue. I can still feel the pang of jealousy I felt then. I was especially envious of the fact that the discipline was administered at bedtime, over pajamas, an intimacy of cane and bottom that day boys like myself would never know.

I learned why rattan was favored as an instrument of corporal punishment not long afterwards, when I got three strokes from Mr. Jameson the junior school headmaster for scrumping strawberries from a farmer's field. I must have been nine. The last thing I saw before I assumed the time-honored position was other small boys' faces eagerly pressed up against the glass panel in the door. Remembering the brave British officer and my nameless Roman predecessor, I determined not to cry.

Manliness. That night, my mother made me chicken noodle soup. Afterwards, I secretly inspected the marks on my behind in the bathroom mirror.

IT BEGINS QUIETLY AND MODESTLY on the organ, without a hint of the splendor that is to come. Swaying, lightly building,

> *dadadadadadadada dadadadadadadada*
> *dadadadadadadada dadadadadadadada*
> *dadadadadadadada dadadadadadadada*

Then, crashing in on that high F in full-throated fortissimo in glorious unison, the choir.

> *Za-dok the priest*
> *and Na-than the pro-phet*
> *anoin-ted Sol-omon king*

And all the people rejoi-oi-oi-oiced.

Seldom have I been so transported. Except, differently, by the fragile, ethereal beauty of Charles Villiers Stanford's Magnificat in G, the soaring treble solo line sung by my friends, Steve (or was it perhaps Peter?) May, Andrew Potts, who had voices of a quality I did not. Except, differently again, in the rising cadences of Hark the Herald Angels Sing, joyfully belted out by choir and congregation at the Service of Nine Lessons and Carols every Christmastide. *The people that walked in darkness have seen a great light. ... For unto us a child is born, unto us a son is given: and the government shall be upon his shoulder: and his name shall be called Wonderful, Counselor, The mighty God, The everlasting Father, The Prince of Peace.*

Six weeks of summer holidays apart, I sang for my supper in Rochester Cathedral every day for six years from age eight. This paid for my education at what in England is known as a public and everywhere else as a private school. It is supposedly the second oldest in the land, founded by Bishop Justus in 604 A.D.

> ***Sing*** *we then the school of Roffa,*
> *for Roffensians proud are we.*
> *Sing the school of saintly Justus,*
> *first to plant the stately tree.*

Choir practice took place every morning at eight-fifteen before school in the room at the top of Gundulf's Tower, lined floor to ceiling with brown cardboard box files stuffed to overflowing with motets, anthems, masses, Te Deums, Magnificats, Nunc Dimitises, Stanford, Gibbons, Purcell, Tallis, Howells, Palestrina, Byrd. Every weekday at four, Saturdays at three-fifteen, we had Evensong. Sunday it was Matins at ten-thirty, Holy Communion at eleven-fifteen, Evensong at three-fifteen. Christmas Day started with a choir practice at nine. Weddings and funerals, for which we got a half crown or even five shillings each, were extra.

I loved it.

The cathedral is cavernous cold spaces and high windows colored and clear—the long plain Norman stonework of the nave, the narrow stretching upwardness of the quire. It is also intimacies. The mustiness of hassocks worn threadbare by shuffling knees, the shine on priestly cassocks, the smallness of The Book of Common Prayer. The little moveable cards, white on black, that hung on the board by the pulpit that spelled out the Hymns of the Day. The hot tiny crowdedness of the organ loft where if you had a cold and couldn't sing you got to turn the pages and watch the choirmaster's feet and fingers fly, snatching the smooth wooden stops with names like *Diapason* lettered black on ivory. The smell in the vestry, fresh sweat from running from school to make the service on time, the stale odor of infrequently washed robes. The vergers' room at the bottom of Gundulf's Tower, warm as toast from the cast-iron stove in the corner, where one spring when I took to cycling in to swim in the icy school pool at seven in the morning I was allowed to eat my breakfast. Soggy with sardines or tomatoes or eggs, Mum's sandwiches always came in a waxed Sunblest bread wrapper.

Ancient moss on the wooden gate to the cloisters from Minor Canon Row—the sheer *dampness* of England, which instantly floods back the moment I step out of the terminal, sniff the air at Heathrow, walk around the quad at St. Peter's, a great wave of nostalgia.

The cloisters lawn, where I once put a cricket ball through a medieval window. The small sunken garden with the wooden benches where we used to talk to Rusty Willard. An old man with a floral waistcoat and a stick, his face and its prominent nose ruddy with a fine tracery of broken veins and capillaries, he was there in the cloisters every Saturday and we would while away the hours with him between the end of Saturday morning school and Evensong. Rusty always had time for small boys.

Too much time by half, my parents thought. When I proposed to invite him one year to our Guy Fawkes Night bonfire party they were only too happy. Rusty came bearing a large box of fireworks and his usual good cheer. They seemed reassured.

Children live in the same world as adults but are not of it—and vice versa. Just as the child is, and is not, the father of the man. When old Joe Levitt, the irascible stand-in for Robert Ashfield the choirmaster, heard that we had debagged one of our number—chased him and caught him and pulled his trousers and underpants down—he angrily lectured us on the *lewdness* of our behavior. Levitt was disgusted. So was I. At Levitt, in his greasy black suit.

It was *him* who was making something filthy out of it with *his* dirty mind.

I loved Andrew Potts's lithe amber body. We called him Panda. His mother was of mixed race, from the West Indies where Father Potts had a parish as a young man. The cane was a fixture in their household too. The boys, Panda once told me, got it on their bare bums, which excited my usual envy.

When I say that I loved Panda's body, that feeling was intense, unself-conscious, and quite without shame. I wanted to stroke his skin. Just like I wanted to take the pain of the cramps Steve May got in his calves, the agonizing pain he told me his doctor father massaged away, for myself. Children are not asexual beings. There is, though, a world of difference between the child's and the adult's sexualities: and this old Levitt failed to grasp. We misleadingly call it innocence: that part of ourselves we leave behind—or at any rate refigure—in the passage through puberty.

Only the memories trail.

> *The ancient dead have escaped the circle and risen again*
> *and smile in a strange silence.*

Is this why the treble voice is so uniquely affecting, so precariously beautiful? It is quite different in timbre from the female soprano. Only two women I have heard come close. One is Nellie Melba in her 1906 recording of the Bach/Gounod Ave Maria. Coarse as a two-bit hooker in life, she had a voice of unearthly purity, plucking those high notes unerringly out of thin air. The other is Alison Stamp in a translucent performance

The cloisters garden. Rochester, 2001.

of Allegri's Miserere, which the young Mozart supposedly stole from the Vatican, recorded in King's College, Cambridge. The sunlight pierces the shadows. She sounds just like a boy.

Is what touches us, perhaps, something metaphorical—the doomed perfection of a voice that is always on the edge of breaking, its fleeting beauty supported by the slenderest column of air? An intimation of mortality, a walk through the valley of the shadow of death, in the cherubic pipings of a ten- or twelve-year-old child?

I used to go carol singing every Christmas, privateering. In a couple of hours I would make what my father earned in half a week. Women invited me into their houses to sing under their trees, lavished me with candy, cookies, mince pies, coins. Then there came a time, round about thirteen, when I longed for my child's voice to snap. I had already looked in the windows of coffee bars, smoked my first cigarette.

ALWAYS THE BODY: growing out of things, changing, the first hairs between the legs. Now it is the first creakings of age, white hairs that can no longer be ignored flecking the brown. Stiffness in the shoulders when I wake, the bleeding of gums and hemorrhoids. Occasional troublesome murmurings in the chest.

Fifty isn't old, boy! pronounces Dad on the phone from Burnham-on-Crouch, six thousand miles and half a lifetime away. He turned eighty this year. The accent I grew up with grates on me, it sounds harsh to my North American ears. It is the year 2000 and my friend Daniel, the last of the long-haired boys, has been dead more than two years already.

What frightens me most is the prospect of my body unhinging my mind.

Nana made it to one hundred two with her marbles intact. Pa was long gone and so were Nanny, dead from a stroke at fifty-one, and Grandad. I last saw Nana on her hundredth birthday. I flew down to Essex from Glasgow with the largest bottle of gin I could find and the first pictures of her first great-great-grandchild, my daughter Natasha. *Pretty girl,* she approved. *Now don't you be having any more just yet! A man shouldn't have no more than he can afford!* She went on to quiz me on my knowledge of the preservatives, as she called them, you could get to prevent accidents these days. Nana's own last child, my mother's Uncle Lou, arrived unplanned and unexpected when she was already in her mid-forties. The old girl, as Dad called her, used to frighten the life out of me when I was a kid, unfailingly greeting me with the words *And what are **YOU** doing here?* Years later she would send me the occasional ten-bob note saved from her pension with the instruction *Buy yourself a packet of fags.*

The copy of Puck of Pook's Hill that sits on my bookshelf is an accidental survivor of my childhood. It was given to me by Mickey Chance, the head chorister, who took me under his wing. Mickey too is long dead. He blew his mind out in a car around the time the Beatles released Sergeant Pepper. So did my friend Jon Cooper, reaching down for a dropped steak pie while driving his father's Jaguar too fast. He was seventeen. The funeral was held in the cathedral. I remember his mother's stiff gray face. I remember his elder brother Robert's riotous drag queen performance as Lady Bracknell in our school play a couple of years earlier.

A handbag?

I most vividly remember the young soldier I met just that once at Jon's funeral and went for a beer with afterwards at the Marquis of Lorne, his face crisscrossed with stitches, the hitchhiker Jon gave a lift to that night. But I remember little of Jonathan. Or of Mickey, come to that.

Inside the cover, the letters neatly joined-up in a large and loopy hand that bears little resemblance to mine, is written

D. G. Sayer,
1, Dashmonden Close,
WAINSCOTT,
KENT.
3.A. King's School, Rochester.

Above it, using a ruler, I have carefully crossed out

M. H. V. CHANCE.
SILVER BIRCHES,
TELEGRAPH HILL,
HIGHAM,
KENT.

The penciled inscription is faint but still legible. *To D. SAYER.* The third form—I would have been ten.

The initials *M.H.V.,* I unaccountably remember, stood for Michael Howard Victor.

A frequent companion in those days was a boy who lived across the street who was also named Derek, or Durrrk, as it sounded when pronounced by his German mother, a bride brought back from the postwar occupation. I didn't know what to make of her. The War hadn't finished for me. German bombs fell on Wainscott, floating down like colored lights into the dream as I struggled to wake up out of the dream. Durrrk's mom put sugared water on lettuce, not salad cream.

Foreigners weren't too common back then. I recall only two at my school, Kofi Bonsu, black as the ace of spades, a wizard fly half, and (Ben?) Arbenz, who came second in the alphabet after Akester. We knew him as The Yid. Only very much later did I learn what the epithet meant. His parents came from Austria. My mother's cousin Jimmy, who had a gammy shoulder from polio, was another of our family who found his way to New Zealand. He consternated us all when he picked up a Filipina wife en route. Lolita was her name. Nana showed us the pictures.

She's not too brown. On the other hand, she's not too white either. Or was it the other way round?

Two-Way Family Favourites, every Sunday lunchtime on the BBC Light Programme, well into the sixties. Tunes for our boys in Suez, Malaya, Cyprus, BFPO 13, 40, 21. PS I love you.

The whole world changed, I think, around the time my voice broke.

The other Derek went to St. Andrew's, which, he gleefully told me when we were pissing up against a wall one day, was *a dirty school*. Did I know about jam rags (sanitary napkins) and rubber johnnies (condoms)? No, I did not, and nor at the time did I very much want to.

Always the body.

> *We have lingered in the chambers of the sea*
> *By sea-girls wreathed with seaweed red and brown*
> *Till human voices wake us, and we drown.*

STRUGGLING MANY YEARS LATER TO EXPLAIN myself to a woman with whom I was deeply in love though I didn't know it yet, I found myself relating this memory.

We crawled out of the window of Gundulf's Tower, shinned up an iron ladder, crossed a flying buttress on a second ladder with rotting wooden rungs, and climbed over the parapet using three iron hoops set asymmetrically in the stone. Each step in this adventure had its own particular fear. A door, which was always left unlocked, led under the eaves of the cathedral roof. There must have been lighting, weak bare electric bulbs. Wooden catwalks crossed deep shadowed pits, the upper side of the perpendicular vaulting in the quire far below. It reminded me of the Mines of Moria, where Merry—or was it Pippin?—drawn to the darkness against his will, dropped the stone down the well-shaft that brought the orcs and wakened the Balrog.

O blessed Meriadoc! cried Pippin as the fragrance of freshly picked mushrooms arose from the covered basket. Following a bout of yellow jaundice I couldn't eat fried foods for two years. One day when Mum was sick my father's drinking buddy Bert, a small weasely man who had been a navy cook during The War, came over and made her his speciality. It just had to be mushroom omelette. He expertly sliced the fungi, fried them in butter. The smell was heavenly.

We reached the bell tower where thick candy-striped ropes dangled down for the ringers. Another ladder, so steep as to be almost vertical, led twenty feet upward to a heavy trapdoor in the floor of the belfry. The only way to open this trapdoor, if you were eleven or twelve, was to turn around and lift it with your shoulders. This required letting go of the ladder. I was the first, from my generation of choristers anyway, to set eyes on the bells in their giant wheels and touch the hands of the immense clock one hundred fifty feet above the ground.

The quire and transepts were later additions built onto the Norman nave, whose massive circular arches have stood in their place now for nine tenths of a millennium. The roof of the nave, I would guess, is about six feet lower than the roof of the north transept. The parapet around the transept takes in only three sides of a square; the fourth is cut off by the bell tower. To get onto the nave roof you must jump down across the right angle where the nave joins the transept. If you miss you will plummet twenty feet or more onto another roof covering the side aisle of the nave. If you succeed there is no way you can climb back. For these reasons I don't think it had ever occurred to anyone to attempt that ridiculous leap. The west roof, and the two towers at its far end that had doors leading to the clerestory below, remained terra incognita.

One day I jumped. Less because I wasn't afraid to than because I was. The recollection of it makes my stomach churn even now—especially now, when I have two children of my own.

I don't think this particular to-boldly-go was quite what Wittgenstein had in mind in the famous closing sentences of the Tractatus. But for me, at least, there remains a vertiginous connection.

My propositions serve as elucidations in the following way: anyone who understands me eventually recognizes them as nonsensical, when he has used them—as steps—to climb up beyond them. (He must, so to speak, throw away the ladder after he has climbed up it.)

He must transcend these propositions, and then he will see the world aright.

Pure chutzpah. But yes, that *was* me. That is why I communicated the memory to her.

Mythical story. Rochester, 2001.

Let me be more precise. I hadn't given the cathedral roof a thought in thirty years—it was the urgency of communicating myself that suddenly brought the memory streaming back, unbidden.

WHAT, THEN, DOES IT MEAN to say *I remember*?

To remember is not an act of volition, except at the most superficial level—remember her birthday, remember to buy the milk. Remembering is scarcely an *act* at all. I can try to make memories, rig the triggers that will bring them back: the photo album, the home video, the mnemonic devices we use to recall telephone numbers or facts for an exam. But even these memoranda cheat us: in the end it turns out to be the snapshots we remember, not the vacation. If I concentrate hard enough, sometimes I am able to trawl my mind and bring back something I know that I once knew but have since forgotten. But this is not straightforward either. Recently, I went from a tune without words to the unique texture of two voices intermingling in my head—*Was it Frank and Nancy Sinatra?*—to *dadadadadadada I love you,* but the title of the song still eluded me. Something Stupid popped into my mind ten minutes later, when I had given up trying to remember and was thinking of something else. Otherwise—which is to say, most of the time—I can no more summon up memories on demand than I can command myself to forget.

The sense in which it is *I* who remembers is akin to the sense in which it is I who breathes—or who dreams. To dream, I must sleep. Only when I recollect the dream next morning—which does not happen very often in my case—do I make it my own, translating it, of course, into something other in the remembrance. It might almost be more accurate then to say *I am remembered.* Memories flow through me, and it is most certainly not me who is directing the flow.

And yet—it is precisely in that uncontrollable flow that the *I* who remembers is also constituted. We say of a man with amnesia that *he has forgotten who he is.* In this sense the self always *is* a memory. There is an I who can remember only because there is an *I* who is recalled. Who is called back.

I only have one language, says Derrida, *yet it is not mine.*

Burt Bacharach songs are playing on the stereo, making me feel mushy.

PRINCE ANDREY WAKES UP WOUNDED on the field of Austerlitz—or was it Borodino?—and sees the sky. Everything recedes into perspective.

I like vastnesses and the quiet that goes with them. The endless plains of the Serengeti, red earth, numberless animals. The salt deserts between Mashad and Tehran, which I saw just once from a train and never forgot. The pitching gray of the Baltic from the deck of a car ferry from Kiel (was it?) on the way to Copenhagen—sea spray on my face. The high range of Montana, mountains in the hazy distance, roads so empty they have no speed limit, slow freight trains a mile long.

Southern Alberta where the chinooks blow and the wheat fields hug the sky.

The prairie seems featureless at first, but it is not. From the air it is a vast checkerboard, white or brown or brilliant with greens and yellows depending on the season. Once, tired from a twenty-hour journey that began at five in the European morning in Prague, I began to hallucinate and the land beneath me started to turn into a Rothko in motion. When the road is disappearing in a sea of white the line of pines on Highway 597 north of Willingdon stands tall and black and proud. In summer you scarcely notice them, bedazzled by the sun on the canola. Change is slow here and subtle but is felt day by day by anyone who knows its signs.

It is a modernist, even a minimalist landscape. Roads are dead straight and go on forever, habitations few and far between. Landmarks are sparse and modest: a wooden Ukrainian church, its onion dome glinting in the sun; a neatly-tended cemetery behind a white picket fence; a weathered gas station straight out of Edward Hopper's painting; a stone Community Hall in the middle of nowhere. A bend in the road. An unremarkable lake choked with reeds—a bridge across a frozen river—a makeshift sign welcoming you onto Indian land. Long-abandoned railroad tracks. Nodding donkeys sucking up the black oil beneath. Grain elevators, the skyscrapers of the prairies, disappearing now one by one.

No superfluous ornament—no superfluity at all. What is there of humanity takes on added poignancy beneath that enormous ever-changing sky.

There is so much space here that gravity is almost palpable, by the grace of God keeping you from just floating clean off the rim of the planet. Puffy white cumulus clouds march in formation as far as the eye can see, rank upon rank upon rank of them. Out of that limitless blue sky, on summer evenings, the suddenness of thunder, sheet lightning filling the horizon.

A tornado chooses an Edmonton trailer park and leaves twenty-seven dead. It was one of the two biggest events in the history of our city, as unfathomable as the day Wayne Gretzky was traded to the Los Angeles Kings.

Next day the sun shone again. In winter cars die but the sun still shines out of a clear blue sky at thirty below. There is something oddly moving in the flimsy wooden houses with their vinyl siding and their tarpaper roofs that shelter us against this harsh climate, modern teepees built to last much less than a lifetime. As if we recognize that this land may be squatted on but never taken possession of—that we are but nomads passing through.

There are few monuments in Alberta, unless you count the deserted barns and homesteads on the back roads slowly turning to humus.

LONG TALL NARROW LONDON HOUSES, at any rate to a child's eyes. One in Hackney, maybe, but it is so out of focus it is barely a recollection at all— my father's father's house. A furrier's bench, silky off-cuts of mink smooth and soft against the skin. Likely I was never there and remember the furs from later. My paternal grandfather died a few months before I was born, nursed by my mother, hardly much more than a girl then herself.

I do remember my father's mother rather sharply from just one visit— that is to say, I remember her surroundings. Herself I don't recall at all— voice, face, nothing, no matter how hard I try. A mental hospital. Green lawns, white verandas, long corridors with dark lacquered hardwood floors. Hatfield?

> And "Tea!" she said in a tiny voice
> "Wake up! It's nearly five."
> Oh! Chintzy, chintzy cheeriness,
> Half dead and half alive!

The other house was in Fulham, a square behind the gasworks I think with some imperial name. I call my mother in New Zealand and she tells me *Imperial Square at the end of the King's Road, you wouldn't believe how they've tarted up those cottages now, national heritage or something.*

What I remember best about the house in Fulham, though I wasn't there when it happened and it probably didn't happen in that house anyway, was Grandad's mother burning his papers in a fit of anger in the boiler in the kitchen, the ticket that certified he had completed his apprenticeship as a bricklayer. Nanny must have told me the story. I thought it a terrible thing, all those years of work gone up in smoke.

It associates in my mind now with the mad Mrs. Rochester locked up in the attic in Jane Eyre and the retelling of her tale by Jean Rhys in Wide Sargasso Sea—both books I read much later. Was it the memory of my grandfather's mother, dead before I was born, feeding her son's prospects into the boiler that made the pyromaniac Mrs. Rochester so enormously terrifying a figure when I encountered her around the same age at which these events occurred in Grandad's youth—if, that is, these events occurred at all? A sense of déjà vu?

She was a fiery Irishwoman, my mother tells me on the phone.

Where did they come from? I had always remembered it as County Cork. *County Tipperary.*

The only other literary scenes that have had a comparable power to make my flesh crawl—beginning at the back of my neck and spreading like some evil orgasm down my spine—play on exactly that creepiness of a memory we cannot logically have but do. Like somebody walking on your grave, they used to say in England. They occur in the opening chapters of Agatha Christie's Sleeping Murder. The young heroine, who comes from New Zealand, buys a house on the south coast of England, a country she is visiting for the first time. She keeps walking into the wall at one particular point, as if she knew there was once a door there, the memory encoded in her body. She remembers the wallpaper lining a closet as having a particular pattern—and on impulse peels the layers off, until she finds the wallpaper to be just as she could not possibly have remembered it.

At a West End performance of The Duchess of Malfi a line is uttered on the stage and she begins to scream uncontrollably without knowing why.

I visited the house in Fulham once more in my mid-teens, when Grandad took me with him for a trip up to London. He had lucked out in the New Zealand national lottery, spent an afternoon at the races where he put his winnings on an accumulator, turned up trumps again, and come back to England to see his daughter and grandkids. He bought me a Seiko watch. He still called me *darling* or *sweetheart*—odd in so masculine a man. It was the Irish in him, I suppose. Six months later Dad was promising to push him off Beachy Head with a pair of water wings.

When the money ran out, most of it going straight back to the bookies, Grandad went back to New Zealand and took a job as a night watchman in Auckland Dockyard. One of my vividest memories of him is in overalls and cap dizzyingly high up laying the bricks on the chimney for the power station on the Isle of Sheppey, the square canvas bag in which he packed his flask of sweet tea and sandwiches by his side. Not that I ever saw him at work. It was all in my mind's eye. I remember it just like I remember him smashing my seventeen-year-old mother's operatic 78s because she was getting above herself. Just like I remember the Ypres salient and the Battle of the Somme, the siege of Gondor and the victory on the Pellenor Fields.

Larry Ryan, his name. That trip home was the last time I, or my mother, saw him—the last time he saw the British Isles.

> Goodbye Piccadilly, farewell Leicester Square,
> it's a long long way to Tipperary,
> but my heart's right there.

Though I never liked it—I hate the feel of metal straps round my wrist—I felt I had lost more than the Seiko when it went missing in the bathroom of a French campsite some years later. I had exactly the same sadness, intertwined with a disproportionate sense of guilt, when the cheap blue radio my father gave me when I went to university was stolen. A rare gift, the more precious for that.

This time I have no memory of the house or its inhabitants at all, only the egg and chips Grandad and I had for lunch there. It has gone down in my mind as the day I discovered I liked fried eggs after all. Now I eat them with Tabasco.

According to Mum I have mixed up two houses and two sets of people in Fulham: Uncle Albert, Grandad's brother; and Aunt Mag, Nana's sister-in-law, who lived with her son Jim. Which and who I visited with Grandad in 1964 or 1965 I don't know, but the childhood memory is crystal clear. Up, up, up the stairs to Aunt Mag, in black like Queen Victoria on pennies that still turned up in the pockets once in a while in the fifties, the worn head of the widow heavy with grief hanging on way past its time.

Fid. Def. Ind. Imp.

That I do remember, and have pegged all else to it—places, people, and tales told by others, all coalescing in one tall London house that never was.

GOING DOWN FOR AIR ... Round about thirteen, when I first made the acquaintance of James Bond (in Thunderball, with two bullet-holes through the cover), we used to read books for *the dirty bits*.

Adams, Richard The scene in Maia where Meris gets whipped. Her thighs are parted and her buttocks raised by the upturned hands of the wooden idol whose face is leering up her ass and whose oversized penis is stuffed in her mouth as a gag.

I didn't write such salacious stuff, the author of Watership Down did—just as Picasso gleefully painted cunnilingus in both pink and blue, and Courbet the origin of the world in the shape of a cunt. Transmuted by its setting from obscenity into art, the cunt now hangs between opened legs in the Musée d'Orsay in Paris for all the world to gawp back at.

Adjectives Pale, white, trembling, pink, red, black and blue. Seven Steps to Heaven. A bedsit in Clapham Junction with a portable gramophone by the bed. The sublime Miles, a much-loved track I once had on vinyl but traded with the rest of my records for a David Hockney print I then sold to raise the cash to fly to Bombay. Cool sounds to get spanked by—not that I was.

Adverbs Gingerly.

Araki, Nobuyoshi Tokyo Lucky Hole: yet another enterprising book from Benedikt Taschen to stand on the shelf beside Art at the Turn of the Millennium and 1000 Chairs.

The normality of the pictures—and Araki's courage in putting himself in them, his arm round the girls, tickling their giggling clits.

Belt He does it systematically, despite being genuinely furious, with well-distributed, criss-cross blows, under which my thin brown buttocks are soon zebra-striped with dark red weals. ... Alberto Moravia, The Belt, a story in his Erotic Tales, a book picked up I don't remember where or when which has hidden on the top shelf in my office ever since. Having lovingly described her first beating she says she has no desire for another, though *the calamity* as she calls it has since been repeated and she is (so to speak) asking for it now—no, she doesn't want to be misunderstood—

I look at the strip of leather I can just see between the loops of his trousers ... a familiar object with which, when all's said and done, I am not on bad terms.

At the end of the story she finds the belt hanging from a nail he has hammered into the wall on her side of the bed. Inviting her to cross the Rubicon. She ponders—and leaves it hanging there.

At least we can talk about it now.

Birch W. G. Sebald writes in detail about the delicate Victorian poet Swinburne, but not his reputed theft of the flogging block from Eton, in The Rings of Saturn—a curious reticence in so impeccably researched a novel.

It's beautiful she said, admiring the exuberant spray of stinging red flowers she had just imprinted on my naked behind. *A meteor shower.*

Bottom Bum, butt, buns, backside. Sit-me-down (*my humble,* as in Robert Coover's Spanking the Maid). Cheeks (alabaster), hemispheres (quivering), orbs (glowing). I have a weakness for the childish, more feminine *bottom.*

All in the mind. Butler's Wharf, London, England, 2001.

Lost for words between the Latin and the vulgar, my mother used to refer to her privates when we were young as her *front bottom*, hinting an equivalence some might find transgressive.

Hairbrush A scene in an old black-and-white film, Bette Davis I think, from which I remember nothing else. She is sitting at her dressing table doing her hair. They are arguing. He tells her she deserves a good spanking. She stands up and hands him the hairbrush, a slow smile playing across her lips.

Merlin A novel by Robert Nye. *The Lady Igrayne is getting whipped on her bare bottom, and loving it* are the words so far as I remember them.

Rattan *n. 1. Any Malaysian climbing plant of the genus Calamus etc. with long thin jointed pliable stems.*

It was at the end of the eighteenth century, with the opening up of the great European trading empires in the Far East, notably the British and Dutch, that rattan, the quintessential cane-making material, first began to arrive in quantity. It was remarkably cheap—much cheaper than whalebone, which rivals it in most other ways—long lasting, and extraordinarily light and flexible. ...

Kipling on the grass where we abandoned the Theories. A cane as slender and supple as my lover. *Swish Swish Swish* goes the Empire. Affinities, intimacies, loves.

Rousseau, Jean-Jacques Confessions.

Sore Seats The title of a porno magazine with a crudely drawn cover on an East End of London newsstand when such thoughts had not crossed my mind in maybe three or four years, a respite I can only explain by hormones raging in other directions. Stripes lacing a picture-perfect behind. I was twenty, in my final year at Essex, working the summer with Boardman's Removals in Stratford where my Auntie Minnie's husband Bill (as distinct from my father's eldest brother Uncle Bill, a furrier like his father) was foreman.

The sudden reminder reduced me to jelly for two days. I did my best to conceal it. Had I listened then to the urgings of my body, my life would likely have been very different.

Six months later I was married.

Verbs Swish, slice, snake, sting, sear, cut, blaze, burn, smart, *gloooooow*.

Welts, like huge throbbing sausages. Fleshly reminders that underneath your neatly pressed pants, your pretty yellow skirt, is a freshly spanked bottom. Who, what, where would we be without our clothes?

Points de capiton. Hooks snagging the nearly fifty-year-old man who smokes Camels to the nine-year-old boy in the playground, the four-year-old braggart in the rightaway, in an improbable litany of eternal returns.

Do I dare to eat a peach?

THERE ARE OTHER WAYS TO MEASURE the closeness between Tobermory and Penang. *How do I love thee?* Let me count the strokes.

The Home and Colonial. India Pale Ale. Burma cheroots. Singapore Sling, invented in the Long Bar of the Raffles Hotel where the peanut shells litter the floor. G & T, the Bombay gin watered with quinine-laced tonic to ward off malaria in saloon bars the length and breadth of the Home Counties. Major Grey's Chutney, Earl Grey's Tea. Kandy, Darjeeling, Simla, all shipped home in plywood chests out of which my father jerrybuilt cupboards for the kitchen when he and Mum were first married. Bengal Lights, the long matches you could buy in the weeks leading up to Guy Fawkes Night that flared red and blue and green round the bonfire,

> *Remember, remember the fifth of November,*
> *Gunpowder, treason and plot.*

Uncle Lou used to come down from time to time with the malarial shivers, a souvenir of wartime days with the Somerset Light Infantry in India and Burma. A less likely soldier is difficult to imagine. He lived for his greenhouse and the one day a year when he got to perform in drag on the London stage for the Boy Scouts' Gang Show. When I think of Lou it is hair brylcreemed back, pipe in hand, *Strolling, just strolling, By the light of the silvery moon.* He lived with Nana and Pa till he was past forty when he suddenly upped and married a large woman named Lil who had boys of her own. There were sniggers.

> *Run, rabbit, run rabbit, run, run, run.*

Jennifer and Clarissa, the Two Fat Ladies with voices full of Victoria plums, prepare an English breakfast of kippers and kidneys and kedgeree washed down with copious cups of tea. *By roads not adopted, by woodlanded ways,* they ride on motorbike and sidecar to the home of the British Army to cook for the officer corps, ghurkas in attendance. Betjeman country, this—

> *Miss J. Hunter Dunn, Miss J. Hunter Dunn*
> *Furnish'd and burnish'd by Aldershot sun.*

Surely one of the most erotic poems in the language. But it is a very local, intensely English eroticism—one expects the vicar to show up any moment looking just like Hugh Grant with the floppy hair and the loopy smile in Sirens—

> *Love-thirty, love-forty, oh! weakness of joy,*
> *The speed of a swallow, the grace of a boy,*
> *With carefullest carelessness, gaily you won,*
> *I am weak from your loveliness, Joan Hunter Dunn*

—a queerly English eroticism, with just the faintest smidgeon of la vice anglaise. *Oh! strongly adorable tennis-girl's hand!* We might be forgiven for thinking the word *gaily* had already taken on the connotations it was to assume some decades later on the other shore of the Atlantic, where they like things to be black and white. An identity, an exclusivity, a one thing or the other. But no.

> *On the floor of her bedroom lie blazer and shorts.*

Sunday breakfast, Dad's fry-up at 1 Dashmonden Close or 6 Medway Road, was less fancy than Jennifer and Clarissa's, but as a treat with the bacon and eggs and sausages we would sometimes get lambs' kidneys. Ah, *the fine tang of faintly scented urine.* On the table was HP Sauce, compounded of the Houses of Parliament, malt vinegar, dates, refiner's molasses, tomato paste, tamarinds, garlic, and spices in the square bottle with the white cap that hasn't changed in fifty years. The same Indian trinity provides the kicker in that most English of condiments, invented in 1830 by two Worcester pharmacists to soothe the palate of a local nobleman homesick for Bengal, the Original and Genuine Lea and Perrins Worcestershire Sauce—

> *tamarinds and garlic and spices!*
> *tamarinds and garlic and spices!!*
> *tamarinds and garlic and spices!!!*

—a chorus-line for an English Wizard of Oz as we all skip on down the primrose path to the everlasting bonfire with Clive at Plassey with Gordon at Khartoum with Wolfe on the Plains of Abraham, with The Famous Five and The Secret Seven, with Harry Wharton and Bob Cherry and Frank Nugent and Hurree Jamset Ram Singh, with Lou and Lil and Miss J. Hunter Dunn, doing the Lambeth walk.

Dyb dyb dyb
dob dob dob
Akela we'll do our best,
won't *we?*

Fancy a cuppa? Nary a tea leaf ever grew on the chalk Sussex Downs where Puck interrupted Dan and Una's midsummer night's dream with his wondrous pageant of England's mongrel history, a riot up and down the globe. Rudyard Kipling lived for a time in Rottingdean—I remember the strange name from childhood holidays at Seaford—an impression of nondescript respectable villas crowding the hillside. How many corpses sleep beneath those herbaceous borders, awaiting their Miss Marple?

I am sick o' wastin' leather on these gritty pavin'-stones,
An' the blasted English drizzle wakes the fever in my bones;
Tho' I walks with fifty 'ousemaids outer Chelsea to the Strand,
An' they talks a lot o' lovin', but wot do they understand?
Ship me somewheres east of Suez, where the best is like the worst,
Where there aren't no Ten Commandments an' a man can raise a thirst;
For the temple-bells are callin', an' it's there that I would be—
by the old Moulmein Pagoda, looking lazy at the sea.

On a clear day, from Beachy Head, you can see New Zealand.

I rented a bicycle in Tobermory and flew over high moors past long cleared crofts to Calgary, a slip of shining sand on the very edge of the western ocean. From Calgary it is a fast hour's drive to the Scottish turrets of the Banff Springs Hotel, the jewel in the crown of the Canadian Pacific Railway.

The Nawab of Pataudi knocking them for six at Lords—ever the English gentleman that Harold Larwood was never. But it was the Nottinghamshire miner as won us the Ashes with his bodyline bowling Down Under.

Ancestral memories, these. The Empire—a music hall, a variety theatre.

The Hillman is waiting, the light's in the hall,
The pictures of Egypt are bright on the wall.

AFTER SEX, SHE SAYS, *I think of High Windows. You know, just a couple of kids fucking.* I remember the poem, and the book it came from, one of those wafer-thin Faber and Fabers I thought so intellectual at sixteen.

> *When I see a couple of kids*
> *And guess he's fucking her and she's*
> *Taking pills or wearing a diaphragm,*
> *I know this is paradise*
> *Everyone old has dreamed of all their lives—*
> *Bonds and gestures pushed to one side*
> *Like an outdated combine harvester,*
> *And everyone young going down the long slide*
> *To happiness, endlessly.*

I am not young, nor really is she, and what we have is more complicated than happiness. But I know what she means. I think. Or maybe Larkin's poem resonates with me for quite different reasons that come together in the moment. It isn't just that (as she assures me) the lines that furrow my face disappear after sex and she briefly forgets the million and one responsibilities she owes to herself and others—that once in a way we are just two carefree kids enjoying ourselves again. There has always been that occasional miraculous understanding between us, punctuating the pomposities with which we are surrounded, letting slip gales of laughter. Enjoying ourselves. At ease with ourselves as neither of us has ever been able to be with anyone else.

You are like my own skin, she once told me.

My beloved student.

Everyone old has dreamed of all their lives. As I am doing now, perhaps. Philip Larkin can be a sour old bastard. But how sublimely the poem ends, leaping from here to eternity:

> *Rather than words comes the thought of high windows:*
> *The sun-comprehending glass,*
> *And beyond it, the deep blue air, that shows*
> *Nothing, and is nowhere, and is endless.*

Beyond the glass the sky. The same blue sky we see reflected back at us in the gigantic eye that fills the canvas in Magritte's The False Mirror.

There is the word *pipe* and the painted image of the pipe, neither of which actually is a pipe. Somewhere beyond, outside the picture, there are real pipes from which the word and the image derive their solidity—

On a clear day. Beachy Head, Sussex, England, 2001.

yet to which neither the word nor the image ever adequately corresponds. You cannot smoke the word, tamp down the tobacco in the image. Still a pipe is a *pipe*, not just a meaningless assemblage of wood or clay. It has a name. It conjures up images. Tommies smoking in the trenches, Pa and Uncle Lou smoking in the front room in Sittingbourne, Merry and Pippin smoking in the wreckage of Isengard. C. S. Lewis and J. R. R. Tolkien smoking in their rumpled tweed jackets with the leather elbow-patches as they dream old worlds together in the snug in the Eagle and Child in Oxford where I drank once with Philip and Daniel. Ripped out of these cascading significances it wouldn't begin to be a pipe either, would it now?

If I close my eyes I can hear that quizzical, ever-so-slightly mocking chuckle in Dan's voice—the one that likely cost him tenure in Arizona. He could be in the room with me now, standing, as he usually contrived to do, somewhere slightly on the edge. But he is not.

The endlessness of the sky, the endlessness of language—I could be confected of every song I have ever heard, every landscape I have glimpsed from a train or a truck or a plane, every morsel of food I have ever put in my mouth, every book I have read, every kiss, every touch. But I am not. I could so easily dissolve into the vastnesses—fly through high windows like Chet Baker and float clean off the rim of the planet. But I do not.

I do not, because this here is *not* a pipe—however much it may resemble one.

Our memories are not the things we remember. The things we remember no longer exist. We compose ourselves out of the traces those things have left in us—figments snagged in the net we cast over the tumult of our lives as they ineluctably and forever escape us.

Blue skies, nothing but blue skies. Empires on which the sun never sets. And at the center of Magritte's eye, a great gaping black hole. La condition humaine.

The illusion of identity—being in denial.

AH LOVE, LET US BE TRUE *to one another.* ...

The opening line I left out when I quoted the last stanza of Matthew Arnold's Dover Beach as the epigraph to the closing chapter of Capitalism and Modernity. Why? Without that line, the poem loses its balance.

I am home alone tonight, listening to Tethered Moon's Chansons d'Edith Piaf, the latest in my Winter & Winter collection. She was the only one who ever remarked on my betrayal of Arnold's poem, a puzzlement of anger and sadness in her eyes that came straight out of her love for me long before we dared think of becoming lovers. When we still had that little piece of ivory, as I tried so hard to make it, defining her times and spaces, confining my feelings within four office walls.

I hunt down Winter & Winter CDs, much as I did matchbox tops or rocks and minerals as a kid, as much for their feel and look as for the music: the sturdy colored cardboard covers lined up like miniature volumes on the shelf, the quirky artwork of the inserts, the way the disk fits snugly into its pocket. There is something anachronistically handcrafted about them. It was on a Winter & Winter CD, Lust Corner—Noel Akchote, Eugene Chadbourne, Marc Ribot—that I first encountered the work of Nobuyoshi Araki. Sixteen photographs. A bony girl lying naked on her side with her hair strewn out across the sheet, a creeper lacing a wall, a single flower shot in dark silhouette against a cloudy sky. When I discovered Araki's fascination with Japanese bondage I liked him still the more. What is so compelling in his photographs is their matter-of-factness. They present, rather than represent. They draw no conclusions.

My love she speaks like silence,
without ideals or violence.
She doesn't have to say she's faithful
yet she's true like ice like fire.

L'Accordéoniste, La Vie en Rose, Sous le Ciel de Paris. There is nostalgia aplenty in these tunes—just as there is in the out-of-focus, rainy photo on the back cover of the CD. If the Low Countries are frites mayo and mists and tobaccos that smell like a candy store, Paris is merguez and couscous and harissa amid the falling leaves of a wet autumn. Slippery gleaming cobbles. The perfection of a plate of green beans with fresh butter—all I could afford at Robert Vattier, one of those legendary twenty-four-hour restaurants at what used to be Les Halles where meat porters in bloodied aprons rubbed shoulders with the après théatre crew at two in the morning. The counters were zinc, the oysters heaped high on cracked ice in baskets outside, and I was barely eighteen.

They return once in a way to the simplest possible statement of the melody. Masabumi Kikuchi plays such passages with infinite tenderness. Everything hangs on his phrasing, his timing, the unbroken line. Gary Peacock plucks at the strings of the heart, his bass the very soul of Le Petit Monsieur Triste. The little sparrow, her Paris—we need no more to beam us straight back. But the music takes us places Piaf would never have gone, too. Kikuchi turns her tunes inside out, probing, questing, trying on textures and colors and hues. He stumbles, loses his way, finds unexpected routes home, hums, mumbles, snarls along with his piano. Discords snag the flow, rhythms slide and shimmer between the instruments. Holding it all together is the flawless delicacy of Paul Motian's drumming. He never seems to lay down a beat, nor does he ever miss one. It is not Piaf I want to listen to in these songs. Not tonight. Tethered Moon get to the heart of the matter. Three old New York jazzmen who weren't even there.

The eternal return of the never-quite-the-same. This is what Richard Wagner was trying to do with his Leitmotiven, create a figure whose repetition instantly recalls a character, a situation, a mood—yet is utterly novel in its every occurrence, a part of now not then.

How can identity be sustained when we change all the time, when transience is the very condition of our existence? *Yet it is.* Music captures what is almost inexpressible in words, this continual warping of time into being.

Eternal returns. Rue de Rivoli, Paris, France, 2002.

Dan laughs as he catches me unawares, my body moving back and forth as the juke-box plays through the long intro to Shine on You Crazy Diamond, twenty-four again. Oxford, whenever. Now I'll never be able to hear that tune without thinking of his smile.

Oh yes, a kiss is still a kiss, a sigh is still a sigh.

WE COME INTO THE WORLD HARD-WIRED for recurrences, make our way through it freighted with the irresolutions of past lives. I have an uncomfortably sharp memory of myself at twenty-four, tongue-tied and shifting from foot to foot in The Three Tuns in Durham when Philip Abrams tried to show off his star graduate student to some visiting American professor. It was the same constriction in my throat that had led Robert Ashfield not to trust me to sing any more solos fifteen years earlier. The same kindliness in their voices, the same disappointment in their eyes as I choke. A promise unfulfilled, whether I had given it or not.

I faced the village policeman in his uniform across the living room table when he came to interview me about the accident the day before. I had been too scared to tell my parents. I was already trying to forget the young man lying unconscious on the tarmac, the people rushing out from Rodney Andrews's house as I furiously peddled away. Acknowledging my fear, the constable spoke softly.

It is an event I find difficult to place in time. I remember nothing of Rodney save his name and the fact that he was a pupil at Wainscott County Primary School like me. His house was set back a little from the road that led from Frindsbury to Wainscott down the hill past the Sans Pareil, *The San* that caused so many rows especially on Sunday lunchtimes when Dad never seemed able to get home by one-thirty and the roast always got spoiled. New Zealand lamb. It took me a long time before I understood why Mum refused to do the sensible thing and time lunch for when the pubs shut.

Beside Rodney's house was an alleyway lined with elderberry trees that provided a shortcut into the housing estate where we lived. New houses were still going up. Mud, puddles, piles of bricks, scaffolding to climb and swing from after the workmen had left for the day. I would guess I was around seven. I sang for a while in Frindsbury parish church before I became a probationer in the cathedral choir. One night I cycled back from choir practice through that alleyway in the midst of what I remember as the most violent storm I have ever seen—probably because I remember it just as I saw it, with the eyes and inexperience of a child. An electrical storm, frighteningly without rain, the sky white with lightning, the horizon flaring red as the oil refinery goes up in flames fifteen miles away on the Isle of Grain.

The funny thing is that I remember it as a *tricycle* I was riding when the motorbike swerved to avoid me. The shortness of my legs, that couldn't pump fast enough, the closeness to the ground. So I could have been as young as five.

It would be untrue to say that the young man lying on the tarmac has haunted me ever since. The memory unexpectedly came back to me two or three years ago. But he troubles me now.

Did I kill him?

And if I did, was it in any meaningful sense *I* who was responsible for his death—a little boy on the other side of the ocean, riding into the road without looking, the best part of half a century ago?

A few weeks back I plucked up the courage to ask my mother what happened. It took her a while to recall the incident at all. (*Or did she remember only too well what she hoped I had forgotten, and was thinking what to say?)* She assured me the man was hospitalized but fine. He came from the village, she said. And, she added firmly, it was a bicycle I was riding, not a tricycle.

The name Rodney Andrews meant nothing to her. I cannot but notice that she remembers the people and places of her own childhood very much better than she does those of mine. She is getting old—cracks in the familiar voice on the telephone—and I find it difficult. The mother I remember is so vibrant, so pretty, so young. All the other kids envied me.

Names, to which I cannot attach faces, float out of the mist. Dave Mortley, Tom Hanks—can it really have been *Tom* Hanks? Or was it Tom somebody else and just the Hanks I've got wrong? Tom Smylie maybe. Certainly there was a Hanks's Pond, where we used to catch long slimy ribbons of frog spawn and tadpoles in jam jars with handles made of string. But they might not have been Hanks's Gang, the village kids who kidnapped me once and made me take my trousers down and pee. They ordered me to *shit* too, but I blubbered instead because I didn't know what the word meant. I heard *ship*. They soon got bored with their game and let me go. Was I six? Once, just once, I ran first across The Field that separated our estate from the village shouting *Charge, men!* and all the other boys followed me. I dreamed of a gang of my own.

The long grass was brushing my legs. Just like in the Lucinda Williams song, the one where she longs to be alone and I get momentarily fearful. So bloody insecure I can get sometimes.

Side of the Road it's called.

The puzzle remains. Whatever the imprecisions of memory—whether mine or my mother's—if I am not who I was at five or six or seven, why should the unknown young man lying on the tarmac, far far away now and long long ago, matter to me at all?

Janus in Old Compton Street, a Soho fixture since I don't know when. Janus was there when I first began to haunt the area in my late teens. Janus was probably there when I first heard the name Soho rumored, back in the time of the spivs.

I saw the naked female derrières that once festooned the window dwindle to one bikini-knickered bottom peeking lonely through a square in the blacked-out glass,

Sugar and spice and all things nice. Old Compton Street, London, 2001.

I saw the best minds of my generation destroyed by madness, starving hysterical naked, dragging themselves through the negro streets at dawn looking for an angry fix, angelheaded hipsters burning for the ancient heavenly connection to the starry dynamo in the machinery of night, times change. My spellchecker redlines *negro* as an error. Howl doesn't electrify me as it did at seventeen. Now the storefront is painted completely black and the sign on the door warns of possible offense to those who might inadvertently enter. Fat chance. As a rule, those of us who frequent this corner of a foreign land that is forever England come here knowing exactly what we are after. To Elizabeth David, Old Compton Street was sugar and spice and all things nice. Me too.

Greek Street, Frith Street, Dean Street where Karl Marx once lived in two slum rooms with Jenny and the kids and Helene the housekeeper he was fucking on the side. Their bastard son Freddie made it into the English working class and died respectable, unlike dear old Dad. Faithful Fred Engels as ever took the rap. I made a kind of pilgrimage once, looking for the old necromancer's finger marks on the ladder of English society, up from Soho past Fred Engels's house by Regent's Park, up, up, up through Kentish Town to Maitland Villas on the fringes on Hampstead, finally coming to rest in Highgate Cemetery. One hundred and fifty years later the tenement building in Dean Street is occupied by the venerable Italian restaurant Quo Vadis and bears a Wedgwood blue commemorative plaque.

New French model, please walk up.

Oh to be in England, where old Marxists never die, they just become Masters of Oxford Colleges. Where famous painters cruise public conveniences round midnight seeking young men to whip their aging butts, and end up hanging in the Tate.

> *Bring me my bow of burning gold.*
> *Bring me my arrows of desire.*

Ancient landmarks cling on among the cappuccino bars—Ronnie Scott's jazz club, Paul Raymond's Review Bar, the neon still flashing out the impresario's moniker on the roof. The Gay Hussar swaggers on, indifferent to the swings and roundabouts of outrageous connotation. I am sure they still serve the same goulash and sour cherry soup as they did thirty years ago. Collets bookstore on the Charing Cross Road, one-time literary outlet of the British Communist Party, has gone the way of all flesh. Remembering my friend Colin Richmond's elegy on his last sixty-six LPs, which he called The Survivors, I feel a twinge of sadness when I discover Dobells too is no longer where I remembered it to be, a hole in the wall opposite Collets, south of Cambridge Circus where George Smiley imagined an England to die for. Colin interwove the old jazz record store so beautifully with his father's death in Sidcup, because that's how it was, without grammar or punctuation. Things hanging half unsaid, things unsayable, you always have to read between the lines. A bus ride over the river, a tale of two cities, worlds apart. It's all history now.

I take her to what used to be the best salt beef bar in London and it tastes like styrofoam.

Back then, I would hurriedly scan the street both ways before scurrying through the door to the back of the store where I would bury my nose in a magazine, all the while casting sidelong longing glances at the canes. I never dared touch them, though. Occasionally I would buy a magazine. Browsers were not appreciated in this temple of the two-faced god. I read them furtively in the anonymity of public places, stuffing them well down into waste bins on railway stations when I was through, feeling dirty and dissatisfied.

Swish, Sting, *ouch!*

The bums were rouged, the characters cardboard, the stories repetitive and predictable. Pornography is as stolid in its structures as any fairy tale. Yet still the signifiers swirl, summoning up specters that rove where they will. It is disconnected details that linger, the pout of a model's behind, a wisp of dialogue, a turn of phrase. I take them out from time to time and burnish them up like Nanny's brasses till over the years their features are all but obliterated.

A rope, a cane, and an ironing board. The back of a hairbrush, solidly Victorian for preference. As beautiful as the chance encounter between an umbrella and a sewing machine on a dissection table.

> Let us go then, you and I,
> when the evening is spread out against the sky.

Violet skies. Rattan dreams.

I HAD NOT MEANT TO WRITE OF RATTANS (I never do) but of paraffin—Aladdin blue and pink—of the terrible heaviness of the square one-gallon can, the metal handle sharp as a knife against the insides of my fingers as my knuckles froze in the bare winter wind. This was one Wainscott errand, to the general store round two corners and up the hill, that I hated, though I was always happy enough to nip out and get Dad a packet of cigarettes. Kensitas? Embassy? Players Weights? I can't remember now.

But I surely loved the paraffin heater, cozy and lethal. I loved hunching crouched over the gunmetal gray cylinder, warming my body, my hands. I loved the smell, the quiet blue flame.

Coldness is inseparable from an English childhood in the 1950s. George Orwell captures all its muscular Christianity in the opening scene of A Clergyman's Daughter. The cold bath Dorothy takes standing shivery naked in a cold enameled basin in a cold English bedroom on a cold and frosty English morning. Healthy drafts through open windows, ice flowers spattering the inside of the pane. Parents in the Indian Civil Service, the playing fields of Eton, the Imperial Police Force in Burma: how much more bloody English can you get?

A Clergyman's Daughter was published in 1935. As I said, the world didn't change till around the time my voice broke.

Between the end of the Chatterley ban and the Beatles' first LP.

In the bleak midwinter,

> *frosty wind made moan.*
> *Earth stood hard as iron,*
> *water like a stone.*

Wind made moan, I like that, almost Anglo-Saxon. It was one of my favorite carols when I was a kid, probably because like so many of the Beatles' songs it was sung in a minor key. So chaste. Only recently did I realize that it was written by Christina Rossetti, she of the ripe juices, juices *that syrupped all her face,* gobbled by goblins.

My Texan friend Wesley likens going down on a woman to sucking on a barbecued duck's leg, a simile that does rare justice to both. *Eat me, drink me, love me.* But sometimes it reminds me—going down, that is—of Seferis's cisterns, the passing scent of an ancient dankness reaching down the millennia, in truth the very origin of the world:

We have no rivers, we have no wells, we have no springs,
only a few cisterns—and these empty—which echo and which
we worship.
A sound stagnant, hollow, the same as our loneliness
the same as our love, the same as our bodies.

And I think of forbidden Catullus and his beloved Lesbia, of Sappho longing long ago on the sun-drenched Mediterranean shore. Of that sublime sculpture in Geoffrey Grigson's book on Aphrodite, Venus with the beautiful backside, youth and beauty turned to stone. I think an eternity of genital kisses, loves locked in bodies that merge all too briefly before they age and wither and die.

What we call society, it occurred to me once—it was when I was in my thirties, I think—is no more than an elaborate device for masking the mortality of the flesh, an everlasting lie of continuity, purpose, point. But this tells only half the story. We do live suspended between here and eternity. The truth is the split and the sadness, the languages beyond that give us voice and the feelings within that we cannot put into words.

How many of our couplings do we *remember*—and if we do remember them, have they not by that act already been transformed into something else, signifiers that float away into the cold blue yonder like all the rest?

We find it strange that once we were able to build
our houses, huts, and sheep folds.
And our marriages, the cool coronals and the fingers
become enigmas inexplicable to our soul.
How were our children born, how did they grow?

Shivering through Monday and Wednesday afternoons on the aptly named Alps, the windswept plateau high above the River Medway that served as the school playing fields, in gym shorts thin as Dachau pyjamas during the January to March hockey season. It is a tasteless simile, perhaps, but that is how I was able to remember the Holocaust. Mengele's experiments, which I surreptitiously read about in a book of my father's, probably the one with the drawing of the British officer getting his buttocks whipped raw in Japan, were unimaginable. I didn't know torture, I didn't know death, I scarcely knew grief. But I could feel all the cruelty of the wind slicing through thin garments across the Polish plains.

Feet up on the old cast-iron boiler in the kitchen in Medway Road, sucking in the first cigarette of the morning before I caught the bus to school. Old Holborn it was then, harsh dark tobacco hand-rolled in sweet brown licorice paper.

The miracle of warmth, which we do not have here in North America, because we never let the cold inside.

I DON'T REMEMBER SHORTAGES and ration books and the Coronation (only the plates and the mugs, though Nanny told me I was there), the unending miserable aftermath of Our Victory in The War. I don't remember poverty. What I do remember is the split and mended beige canvas-covered sofas in Dashmonden Close, the Hillman Minx sitting rusting and overgrown with weeds in front of the garage for two years because there wasn't the money to fix it. Cold meat and chips if there was any meat left over from the Sunday roast, otherwise eggs and chips on Mondays, cheese and onion casserole on Tuesdays, saveloy sausages on Wednesdays.

Was the oil in the chip pan *ever* changed?

Frugality, that's the word. Making ends meet. It was second nature with my father to turn off the immersion heater whenever someone switched it on to heat the water for a bath. Two inches they were allowed during The War.

I swore, when *I* grew up, that there would be no arguments in *my* house over money.

The window is open in a prewar villa in Prague, probably in early December 1991. Billowing clouds of steam condense into rivulets running cold down the pane. I lower myself into the scalding water, gingerly. I feel the goose pimples forming on my arms and shoulders and chest and am startled by the sharpness of the reminder. Suddenly I am back, sloughing off the passage of years, the crossings of oceans. Feeling the icy touch of nylon sheets on my naked flesh in a Victorian bedroom that never knew heat since coal and servants got too expensive and the fireplaces were all boarded up. Diving into the school pool, shadowed by high walls, the water barely above freezing, swimming a fast length at seven o'clock on a chilly May morning.

It almost stopped the heart.

Enameled basins with water jugs still stood sentinel on marble washstands in the Esplanade Hotel annex where we took our family holidays every year through the later fifties until, I would guess, 1961 or '62. (When did Del Shannon release Runaway?) We vacationed annually in Seaford, between Eastbourne and Brighton on the Sussex coast, because employees of the Trust Houses architectural department got to stay there on the cheap.

What my father didn't spend on drink he didn't have. Or so Mum always said, anyway.

Fraying carpets on cracked linoleum. A long corridor, at the end of which, one night after I had been put to bed but not yet to sleep, a door thudded distantly shut. Later that night I dreamed I was trapped under a net, smeared with peanut butter, being prodded and pinched by goblins. I woke screaming, and my mother came. That must have been the first year we were there, when I was making a slow recovery from a surgery more or less obligatory for small children at the time, an operation to remove my tonsils and adenoids.

I fought as they slipped the mask over my face, as Mum's and Nanny's smiles receded into anesthesia, gagged on the smell of black rubber.

The sea was rough enough sometimes to fling pebbles up across the Esplanade and smash windows in the boarding houses and hotels along the front as the wind howled and we hunkered down over tea and chess or whist or rummy and Enid Blytons borrowed from the penny library above Boots the Chemist. Dad taught me to swim in that sea, and I swam in it every day it was calm enough, staying in the water till long after I couldn't stop the chattering of my teeth. By the time my mother wrapped the towel around me I would be shivering uncontrollably and she would tell me off, again.

At a church fete in Seaford I bought Nanny a cake server made out of mother-of-pearl at a white elephant stall. *Are you **sure** you want it?* Mum asked me, rather doubtfully. But I thought it was utterly beautiful, in the way, sometimes, that children do.

Newhaven, five miles or so down the coast, was somehow always warmer, and the crescent of beach abutting the harbor where the ferries sailed for Dieppe was sand, not shingle. We always clamored to go there, Alison my sister and I. But Newhaven lacked Seaford's rough magic—the bleached breakwaters marching into the sea, green and barnacled and slimy below the waterline, sea-smoothed driftwood and bottles promising messages, seaweed that came in ribbons and tangles and clumps, strange shapes and dull watery colors, yellows and browns and olive greens, salty, smelly, with nobbly brine-filled buds, sometimes, that you could pop between your fingers. Lumps of black squishy tar. Shells. Dead things, to be fingered and poked and prodded, sponges and starfish, the white bones of cuttlefish and the carcasses of crabs. Stones for skimming, stones for collecting, stones for chucking at posts and cans and yellow-billed gulls.

I can taste it now.

At Aldeburgh on the Suffolk coast, where my father took me with him on one of his trips away, I happily spent the whole day in solitude combing the deserted winter beach for amber. At Hastings a few years later, where my father found me a job on a construction site after I was suspended from school, I spent January nights disconsolate, scouring the deserted winter beach for Swedish girls before crawling back to a cold bed and Bertold Brecht's Threepenny Novel. Or the poems of poor rollicking drunken Dylan Thomas, with whose legend I strongly identified at the time. *By full tilt river and switchback sea, where the cormorants scud ...*

I can see the sea! I can see the sea!

A SUDDEN RECOLLECTION flashes up from nowhere. Two naked children toweling themselves dry after a bath in front of an open coal fire. Slim white hairless bodies. Me and Alison, in the living room of Dashmonden Close.

What *can't* take you way back when? The tinny sound of the speakers on my new laptop, the only flaw in a postmodern technological miracle, *exactly* recalls the way the Top 20 sounded on my first transistor radio as I illicitly listened under the blankets at ten o'clock on a Saturday night to faraway Radio Luxemburg.

Except for the signal fading in and out.

A couple of years later it was Pirate Radio Caroline, Tony Blackburn spinning disks for his lovely Tessa from a tramp steamer moored six miles off Frinton on the Essex coast.

The first thing the wind hits as it sweeps in off the North Sea is the towers of Essex University.

SHE WAS NOT STANDING IN AN ENAMELED BASIN, Orwell's clergyman's daughter. The water was cold, the morning was cold, and she was shivering and naked all right. But it was an ordinary bathtub Dorothy stepped into, slowly immersing herself in the icy water. Maybe at some point the wires got crossed and I remembered her through all those Degas pictures of women at their toilet I found so erotic later. His horses and jockeys were never half so interesting. She gets irritated with me when I intrude on her showering, but I cannot resist. There is nothing in this world I find so beautiful. The grace of her movements, the inclinations of her belly, her hips, her neck, as she bends to soap herself, throws back her head and lifts her arms to rinse the shampoo from her hair.

Is this perhaps Degas too?

Or maybe the slippage occurred earlier, the bathtub mutating into Seaford's spartan washstands even while I was reading the book, a surreptitious making of Dorothy's masochistic ablutions my own.

Her body had gone goose-flesh all over. She detested cold baths; it was for that very reason she made it a rule to take all her baths cold from April to November.

(He must learn to apply himself to work that does not interest him.)

And it was of course Pippin, not Merry, who dropped the stone down the well in the Mines of Moria. *Fool of a Took!* growled Gandalf. The same imprudent, insatiably curious Peregrine Took who couldn't resist looking into the seeing stone, the palentír of Orthanc, and *almost brought ruin on us all.* But fate moves in mysterious ways. *Maybe even your foolishness helped, my lad!* That was where I started The Lord of the Rings, with volume 3, The Return of the King, and Shadowfax's great ride to Minas Tirith. Pippin huddled in the shelter of Gandalf's cloak as the beacons of war flashed by in the night. *See, there is the fire on Amon Din, and flame on Eilenach; and there they go speeding west: Nardol, Erelas, Min-Rimmon, Calenhad, and the Halifirien on the borders of Rohan.* Such names—I was hooked.

I begged the book from the adult section of Rochester Public Library when I was still in short pants and my face was a couple of inches below the counter. That and Norse myths: Loki who tricked Baldur's blind brother Hodur into killing him and took the sunshine and youth away from Asgard. Then I read The Fellowship of the Ring, and last of all—the library never did get it in, so I knew the end before the beginning and the middle last of all—The Two Towers. I pleaded and pleaded till Nanny bought me all three volumes, in red-bound hard covers, for Christmas. It must have been her last. I have read them countless times—most recently in Czech, in 1992. I reasoned that since I had the whole book in my head in English, it would be a fast track to learning the language.

But did I?

Pippin cries *O blessed Meriadoc!* at the sight of steam rising from a hot bath. I remembered the exclamation aright when I quoted it earlier, but it had nothing to do with mushrooms or my yellow jaundice. It was Frodo who laughed as the fragrance of mushrooms arose from the covered basket given him by Farmer Maggot a few pages previously, before they crossed the Brandywine to Buckland, leaving the black rider on the far bank sniffing for their scent in the mists.

> *Can the black riders **see**?* asked Merry.
> *They themselves do not see the world of light as we do, but our shapes cast shadows in their minds, which only the noon sun destroys; and in the dark they perceive many signs and forms that are hidden from us: then they are most to be feared. And at all times they smell the blood of living things, desiring and hating it. Senses, too, there are other than sight or smell ...*

Then and now, now and then. Is it Tom Waits or me insinuating Tolkien's Nazgul into Sally Bowles's Berlin, cowering before the stairs to Shelob's lair as *that host clad in sable, dark as the night* streams through the Brandenburg Gate? *This way and that turned the dark head helmed and crowned with fear, sweeping the shadows with its unseen eyes.*

The cloth that covered the basket of mushrooms was blue and white gingham check by the way, though as far as I remember Tolkien never actually says so.

What do they mean, these garblings? Do I just have a lousy memory—or is the device, perhaps, optimally configured and functioning properly, continually running in the background, laundering sensations into significances, counterfeiting currency out of the leavings of the past? Can we judge the truth of a memory by its accuracy: as distinct from its sharpness, its poignancy, its capacity momentarily to cohere, to recover, a self, a life?

> *Reading Yeats I do not think*
> > *of Ireland*
> *but of midsummer New York*
> > *and of myself back then*
> *reading that copy I found*
> > *on the Thirdavenue El*

Shall I remember this moment? Los Angeles County Museum of Art, Los Angeles, California, 2002.

Mum tells me I *did* see Grandad once laying bricks high up on a chimney, much as I have described him here. But it wasn't on the Isle of Sheppey, where he worked when I was eleven or twelve. It was in West London, and I was three years old. I also inadvertently slandered him earlier, remembering wrong again. It was not Grandad, Mum says, but my father's father who smashed her 78s. She shows me an old photo of my paternal grandparents. American gothic.

I wake to a warm familiar smell, part musk part baby and utterly unique to her. It clings to her skin. I bury my face in her neck. She spoons against me, her left buttock resting soft against my thigh.

I say *how good it is to have a nice soft girl in my bed again* and she laughs. Shall I remember this moment?

September 6, 2000, the morning after her thirty-fourth birthday.

IN TAHITI, FOLLOWING THE TRACKS of Paul Gauguin, I buy my love a single black pearl with microscopic blemishes, deep and dark as the tropical night sky. The Gauguin Museum, an hour along the coast from Papeete, has no Gauguins. They are all in London, Paris, and New York. White wooden Protestant churches, immaculately looked after, little canopies over the graves.

On the road again. Not exactly voluntarily, but separation, right now, looks a better bet than falling apart.

To India, I remember, I took half a dozen LPs and left them there—Bob Dylan's Highway 61 Revisited and Nashville Skyline, Janis Joplin's Cheap Thrills, a Bessie Smith collection, and two other records I can't recall, one of them maybe the Rolling Stones' Beggars' Banquet—or just possibly it was their Let it Bleed.

For Tanzania I made cassette tapes of mostly dead sopranos, beginning with the beautiful remains of Adelina Patti's voice as recorded in her drawing room in Craig-y-Nos Castle in North Wales around 1905. *Ah, je ris!* Nellie Melba's incomparable trill spinning out for what seems an eternity in a trifling song of Bizet's. The red-headed Ljuba Welitsch running the gauntlet of operatic femininities as Strauss's eighteen-year-old princess with the voice of an Isolde morphs into Tchaikovsky's budding Tatiana. *Ich habe Deinen Mund geküsst, Jokanaan, Ich habe ihn geküsst, Deinen Mund! So* sexy. Berta Kiurina cavorting in the caballetta to Casta diva, the sweetness of Amelita Galli-Curci with the big medieval eyes. *Piangi! Piangi fanciulla piangi!*

The divine Claudia Muzio, not the famous series of records she made for HMV the year before she died, choking out the hopelessness of Violetta's Addio del passato on just one lung, but the fresh-voiced Edisons of twenty years earlier. Two arias in particular I can hear now, her voice melting and limpid, caressing down the years through the crackle and hiss of the old acoustic recordings: Handel's Lascia ch'io pianga, and

Ammogliato from an opera called Zazà by God knows who. Leoncavallo maybe.

I scarcely listened to any of them. I did my time at the Hotel Africana, if I remember right, to the accompaniment of Diana Ross, with and without the Supremes.

Do you know where you're going to?

Very hit and miss, music for traveling with.

JE SUIS LE SPECTRE D'UNE ROSE *que tu portas hier au bal.*

Laissez-faire Mademoiselle Teyte! snapped Debussy. She was young then. Nobody thought to ask her to make her celebrated recordings of French songs for another thirty years, during and after The War. There was a time when my passion for opera got me into trouble with both sexes, gifts of lovingly prepared tapes being mistaken for overtures of another sort. But opera feels wrong these days, all gauze and glitter and suspension of disbelief. It recalls a north-facing living room shaped exactly like a coffin in West Princes Street in Glasgow whose gloom I could never dispel no matter that I painted it gleaming white; a time when all the choices I made were wrong. A pity, because I loved it. The music, I mean.

Maggie Teyte, though, remains the freedom of the prairie—driving alone on the Trans-Canada Highway, hugging tight to the bends, reveling in the power and the space and the solitude—the soaring of her sixty-year-old voice, especially in that song from Berlioz's Nuits d'Été, as I shift down to pass, always on the lookout for the cops.

I lent her this CD years ago, in the time of our little piece of ivory, and she immediately went out and bought it for herself. So now we have duplicate copies, as we do of so much else.

Half my brain and more than half my heart haven't made it to New Zealand yet. What of me is here sleepwalks through the days as if on Prozac, sleeps too soundly at night. The sense of displacement is compounded by this house of transplanted familiarities—a lovely house, as it happens, bright with blues and yellows, overflowing with kitsch and whimsy, snug in its hillside surrounded by Mum's cheerful gardens. Outside the kitchen window sheep graze and lambs gambol in a green English landscape ripe with gum trees, tobacco weed, and bamboos. I am surprised to find a copy of Dad's pen-and-ink sketch of Mermaid Street in Rye hanging on the hallway wall when Mum left him so acrimoniously more than twenty years ago—and I immediately miss its inseparable companion in all the living rooms of my childhood, his drawing of the farm house at Chalfont St. Giles in Buckinghamshire where Nanny and Grandad used to keep their little caravan.

I fell off a gate there when I was three, cutting my head on a flint, and they gave me a tetanus shot in my bum.

Dr. Cox taps my chest. I can still feel the cold of the stethoscope on the skin of my back. Say *Ah*.

Objects disconcert, trailing memories that no longer gel with who I have become. Distances are foreshortened. I am startled by old books with my name in them, The Oxford Dictionary of Quotations (*Derek Grant Sayer*, it says, *September 1965*), The Penguin Book of Contemporary Verse, its pretty yellow cover a little faded now, even my cheerless bedfellow in Hastings, Brecht's Threepenny Novel. I have no desire to read it again. Photographs of my children stand on the bookcase side by side with those of relatives on my stepfather's side I didn't know I had. I'm not sure which seem the more out of place. I flip through The Albatross Book of Verse, awarded me for the Sir Malcolm Stewart Prize for Original Composition in July 1966, and stumble across Theodore Roethke's Elegy for Jane, My Student, Thrown by a Horse. It meant little to me then, at fifteen. Now it distills my uncertainties, clarifies my fears.

A found object.

> *If only I could nudge you from this sleep,*
> *My maimed darling, my skittery pigeon.*
> *Over this damp grave I speak the words of my love:*
> *I, with no rights in this matter,*
> *Neither father nor lover.*

This time, being nearly fifty and knowing better, I carry with me a mixed bag of musical memoranda—Astor Piazzolla, Gidon Kremer, the Kronos Quartet. Dave Douglas's Charms of the Night Sky. Joshua Redman, Joe Lovano, Charlie Haden. Tethered Moon. Lucinda Williams, just in case I get homesick for the times out we have snatched in Banff these fraught two years. Three hours of Tom Waits, two of the brattish British Oasis, one of Richard Buckner, our adopted Edmonton homeboy. The very hip Cibo Matto. I hesitated long and hard before taking Bob Dylan. He doesn't quite seem to belong either, I'm not sure why. Just one of those inexplicable feelings. Finally there is the incomparable Mademoiselle Teyte.

The devil is in the details. As always. There is little here that I knew and still less that I owned three years ago. An act of faith.

> *Reviens, reviens! Ma bien-aimée!*
> *Comme une fleur loin du soleil*
> *La fleur de ma vie est fermée*
> *Loin de ton sourire vermeil.*

GANNETS, GUILLEMOTS, PETRELS swooping down to scoop the fish from the water. Cleats, bowsprits, halyards, Yankees, fo'c'sles, Dorado boxes, lazarettes. This is a *ketch,* Robin explains, with the main mast forward of the mizzen, not a schooner or a yawl. Words I had forgotten or never knew, full of evocation. I marvel once again at the plenitude of language, the sufficiency of vocabularies to create entire worlds.

Maybird, the boat is called, a wooden forty-three footer built in Ireland in 1937. Once the flagship of the Royal Yacht Club at Cowes, it was sailed to New Zealand in the seventies by two architects with their young families on board, a three-year journey meandering through the Mediterranean to the southern seas. Robin had to sell it the year he married my mother when his businesses crashed, leaving them to pick watermelons and hawk inverters around Australia. My sister's husband Darryl bought the yacht when it came on the market again last year so it is back, in a manner of speaking, in the family. *She* is back, I should say. And when I say the family, of course, it is a manner of speaking too. Scattered by divorces, spattered across the globe, we mostly just flit in and out of each other's memories in the usual unreliable ways.

Mum brings me a piece of glass about five inches long flecked with purple on one side and white on the other, shaped like a caveman's club. She walks more stiffly now than when I saw her last, four or five years ago in Edmonton, complains of tinnitus in her ears. It is my first visit to her home in New Zealand, my first meeting with my stepfather Robin.

Do you remember this? she smiles.

Of course I do. I bought it for you in Murano, on a school trip to Italy when I was thirteen. We fall to talking of other sentimentalities. The box I bought her from the shop in Rochester High Street with weekly installments from my pocket money when I was nine or ten. I had remembered it as a glass animal, the first of many—but maybe those I got for Nanny.

The demonstration—I even remember the date, March 17, 1968—outside the US Embassy in Grosvenor Square in London. *I wasn't there,* I repeat. What I remember is my regret at missing out on the action. *I watched it on the TV, with you. Don't you remember? When Jem's Sue went down under a policeman's horse?*

I remember Mum's hand clapped with horror over her mouth in the living room in Medway Road even if she doesn't, clear as if it was yesterday. ***Don't I?***

The fight in a café in Afghanistan, when I was cut in the head by a flying chair. I have no recollection of any such fight at all, though I *almost* remember it when Mum starts talking about it, like a word on the tip of my tongue that just won't come. She suddenly woke, she says, that night, and *knew* I was in trouble.

Oh yes, Afghanistan. Pathans shouldering their rifles, women behind head-to-foot veils, tablets commemorating the British dead set into the vertical walls of the Khyber Pass. Kabul, Kandahar—a name to conjure with, straight out of C. S. Lewis's The Horse and His Boy—Herat, where I kicked my heels for three days waiting for a visa to cross the Iranian border and drank scalding black tea sitting on a stone bench in the dusty sun. But that is *all* I remember, the tea and the bench. James Nachtwey's dreadful photo of Herat unnerved me when I encountered it last year having all but forgotten the very name—a family cooking on a fire in the ruins of what was once their home, a town where the houses don't have roofs any more. Everything is bathed in that lurid red-orange glow through which I once long ago imagined Mordor.

We anchor the boat in fifty feet of water for a lunch of tea and cold chicken sandwiches, unzip and piss over the side. The radio is on, the year is 1963. They play Gene Pitney's Twenty-Four Hours to Tulsa, the Crystals' Da Doo Ron Ron. *I wanna be your man* howl the Rolling Stones, and I have a sudden flashback of my father, beside himself, spitting *Animals!* at the TV. I smile at Penny, an Englishwoman of my own age, all cashmere and gumboots and Benenden vowels. *You know, this was the exact moment, this song, when the world started going to hell in a handbasket.* She laughs. Spidery lines around her baby-blue eyes, brittleness beneath the poise. *If you don't do it now, you never will,* Mum tells her. Penny is about to depart for Toronto where her sister is starting a catering business, leaving behind a man and what used to be my mother's house in Kerikeri. The Mexican pines Mum planted there twelve

A sign. Houhora, New Zealand, 2000.

years ago are over thirty feet tall now, the jacarandas that line the drive-
way starting to reach for the sky.

Mum left Dad at the same age as Penny's, the same age as mine, at
forty-nine.

The last time I saw jacaranda trees was seventeen years ago in Tanzania, where they surrounded the old tobacco barn David Phillips had
converted into a home on his dairy farm in Iringa. David must be long
gone. He played me 78s of Caruso and Gigli on a wind-up phonograph
by the soft light of kerosene lamps.

I stretch out on the deck forward of the cabin, wrapped up in the
bright yellow windbreaker she bought me when we were last in Banff,
leaving the women to talk. I am grateful for the broad-brimmed bush-
man's hat I bought to amuse her shading the sun from my eyes. Low
sunlit hills light the shoreline, basalt columns rise vertical out of the
water like a miniature Giant's Causeway. The wind is southerly, blowing
cold straight from Antarctica, the sea choppy with white horses. The sky
is a deep blue, the waves phosphorescent. I drift away, miles away, as the
sunshine dances on the water.

That evening I call home, burble on about my day. Hers was shitty, and we end up rowing. *Why am I here, while she is there?* The bubble bursts, the moment is lost. I know it is temporary, this intimation of contingency, but it pierces to the core.

Why do I feel so bloody fragile? I try to lose myself in the Penguin with the yellow cover that was once upon a time mine, but find no consolation there. Just the low-key and somehow very British despair of Louis MacNiece, all the sadder for its banality:

> *It's no go my honey love, it's no go my poppet;*
> *Work your hands from day to day, the winds will blow the*
> *profit.*
> *The glass is falling hour by hour, the glass will fall for ever,*
> *But if you break the bloody glass you won't hold up the weather.*

SKINNY-DIPPING A COUPLE OF WEEKS LATER from my brother's speedboat at The Noises, a minuscule group of islands off Auckland's east coast. It helps break the ice. *An ax for the frozen sea within me.* I haven't seen Neil in fifteen years, not since Nana's hundredth birthday. We have a good week rediscovering one another, swapping reminiscences and doing boyish things. Elvis belts out on the stereo of his very loud Holden V8, *You were always on my mind.* He keeps playing that song. There is a peculiar tenderness between us, still. I say still, though I don't actually recall it having been there when we were children.

I was six and three quarters when Neil was born. Mum had a bad pregnancy, and Alison and I were sent away. Alison got to stay with Nanny. I was shipped off to stay with the family of some colleague of Dad's, in Bushey in Hertfordshire. They had two boys, three or four years older than me. They had built a tree house at the end of the garden with hammers and nails and real planks of wood. I was not so much bullied as made to feel very small and always in the way.

I should have been the one staying in Sittingbourne getting Nanny's bosomy hugs, the apple of her eye.

It is Guy Fawkes Night in Napier, next door to Hastings, just up the road from Clive. We drove down from Auckland, Mum, Robin and I, passing the Khyber Pass and the Bombay Hills. *New Zealand,* Mum says, *is more English than England.* I know exactly what she means. It is an

Englishness pared to its essentials that is etched on this landscape, a Boy's Own adventure with the world for its stage. Long ago detached from their loci of origin the totems of identity mutate and miscegenate to create an Empire of simulacra, girdling the globe. Sandringham neighbors Balmoral, the Coromandel Peninsular lies on the Firth of Thames.

There are war memorials everywhere. Beside a ramshackle rugby stadium in tiny Kohukohu in the Hokianga, a homespun Arch of Remembrance is inscribed with the dates 1914–1918 and thirty-five names. On Piha Beach two tablets have been hammered into Lion's Rock, which crouches gigantic on the sand, ever ready to spring out over Abel Tasman's sea in defense of king and country. In Paeroa field guns frame a gay soldierly mural beside an advertisement for a farm equipment supplier. In Rotorua, where I went to see the volcanoes and hot springs because Grandad sent me specimens from there for my rock collection all those years ago, the monuments are set out orderly amid the lawns of Government Gardens—the Boer War, The Great War, The War.

The Croquet Club pavilion has a green tin roof whose sweep is faintly reminiscent of a Chinese pagoda.

The mother of all war memorials must be the Auckland Museum. Above every window, carved into the gray stone, is the name of a battle, a campaign, most of them inexorably slipping now out of memory into history—Guadalcanal, Crete, Malaya, Vietnam. Gallipoli gets a tablet to itself: the date of landing, *26th day of April 1915*, followed by a list of names—*Shrapnel Gully, Walker's Ridge, Quinn's Post, Russell's Top, Krithia, Sari Bair, Pope's, Lone Pine, Chunuk Bair, Apex, Kaiajik Aghala, Hill 971.* That's all. What will these names mean when there is no longer anyone left alive to remember them? I cannot say. I know only that they are capable of bringing the same overwhelming choke to my throat as Keep the Home Fires Burning or We'll Gather Lilacs in the Spring Again. Are we then but hostages to the signifier, eternally tugging at the heartstrings, dragging us back to where we never were to begin with?

I find what I am not looking for on the other side of the world, carved on a limestone wall between Rossignol Wood and La Signy Farm.

Bapaume.

MY GRANDFATHER IS BURIED somewhere across the harbor in Devonport in an unmarked pauper's grave. Mum drives me down the street where he lived, Hastings Parade, but she doesn't know which house was his. It doesn't really matter. They are all pretty and quaint, all pastels and gables and finials, a fitting habitat for a man who dreamed of populating the southern hemisphere with garden gnomes. Grandad died, Mum tells me, in the North Shore Hospital at seventy-three—a good age, considering what the brick dust had done to his lungs. She was only told a month later when they tracked her down to Burnham-on-Crouch. By that time his earthly remains were long disposed of. There is no stone to lay flowers on, nothing tangible to remember him by, yet everything conspires to bring him back. I find a twelve-inch ruler in a gift shop in Paihia in the Bay of Islands, exactly the same as the one I had forgotten he gave me, inlaid with little colored squares made of the different native timbers of New Zealand. When I get home I shall frame it and hang it on a Canadian wall.

She e-mails me, much amused at the photos I sent her of Neil's and my brotherly D. H. Lawrencing in the Hauraki Gulf. *The truth is, I find it worrisome that your family jewels are exposed but also kinda erotic—*

Don't ask. Mangonui, New Zealand, 2000.

because I see your butt floating on water—and it would be so pretty if there were stripes on the butt.

Naughty girl!

Heinz baked beans, fish and chips at the country club, a dog-eared edition of Antony and Cleopatra covered in scribbled annotations for an A Level sat in Singapore nearly twenty years after I studied the same play for the same examination in King's School, Rochester, Kent. Every last word of Pride and Prejudice. The Beano and The Dandy, South Pacific and Jamaica Inn. Sherry trifles and Wesleyan hymns, Cliff Richard and Enid Blyton. And yes, navy-blue knickers and rattan canes. The things that connect us. Indelible as that large brown mole on my backside she likes so much, which, Mum tells me, Grandad had too.

Do I look like him? Sometimes.

If you can read this without any sense of irony perhaps you will understand. It is written in stone, to echo down the ages, beneath bas-relief figures of their majesties King George and Queen Mary on a Maori memorial in the government gardens in Rotorua:

Erected
by the
Arawa Tribes
in perpetual
remembrance
of their sons
who in the
Great War
loyally upheld
the cause of
their God
their country
and their King
1914—1919

Rockets rise from back yards, catherine wheels fizz, jumping jacks sputter. It is cold and drizzling, exactly as I remember remember the fifth of November. I call home to my neater sweeter maiden from a blue and yellow telephone box at the uttermost end of the earth, just across the street from a Chinese chippy, happy as Larry.

I FIRST VISITED ITALY on that school trip at thirteen, when I bought my mother the Murano glass off-cut on a day trip from Venice. That was my second journey abroad, my first being our one and only foreign family holiday at Lloret del Mar on the Costa Brava the summer before. From that holiday I remember only, but vividly, the storm that blew up when we took a trip on a converted fishing boat down the coast, the boat tossing and the sailors laughing as they used their hands to clap up an impromptu flamenco dance; the shooting gallery where you aimed at a knob on a little door, and if you hit it a small keg popped out on runners and the stall-keeper poured you a miniature tot of brandy; the signs everywhere advertising Fish and Chips and Tea Like Mum Makes It; and my xenophobe father, to my astonishment, tucking into tins of smoked baby octopus and washing them down with rough red wine in a base-ment bar he derisively referred to as Smoky Joe's. I was last in Italy in the mid-1970s, a shoestring holiday in a beat-up Triumph with our friends Ben and Thea, from which my wife and I bailed out early, returning home alone. It was the one country in Europe, I said then, that I would love to spend more time in. When the chance came up a quarter-century later to teach for a semester in Tuscany, I grabbed it with both hands.

The landscape, the history, the buildings, the art.

Now I wonder whether I have not been hijacked again by nostalgia— drawn back not by Italy itself but by a memory of what it once upon a time stood for, when I was somebody different, and the world was a smaller—or do I maybe mean a larger?—place.

The guidebooks call Cortona a hill town with reason. Circled by ramparts perched high above the Val di Chiana, it has a bird's-eye view of any approaching armies and plenty of time to slam the gates shut. There is one level street, the Via Nazionale, which leads two hundred meters from the Piazza della Repubblica before it abruptly hits the wall at—where else?—the Piazza Garibaldi. So European. So *fucking* Europe-an. Everywhere they have them on this claustrophobic old continent, their Národní třída, their Náměstí republiky, their Masarykovo nábřeží, as their counterparts were called in Prague. Cusina typica, one local trattoria proudly advertises itself. Not a single Chinese, or Indian, or Thai, not even a KFC or a McDonalds. I haven't seen a face that isn't white since I have been here. It is out of season—winter, the time, my American colleague tells me, when Cortona finds its identity again.

I find myself niggled by incorrect thoughts, like that fascism always fared best in old countries that lost out in modern struggles for overseas empires, countries where the otherness of others had a chance of being sustained because they were never around to dilute the culture and pollute the blood. Countries where they don't eat vindaloo or couscous or nasi goreng. Ein Volk, ein Reich, ein Führer.

Give me my Chinese smorgasbord and Mexican sushi any time.

The buildings are four and five stories high, the streets too narrow for two Fiats to pass. Every inch of space has been occupied for centuries if not millennia. Houses turn their backs to the street, their meter-thick stone walls grudgingly pierced with high shuttered windows. The effect is more canyon-like than anything in Manhattan. I miss the openness, the all-forgiving amnesia, of North America, where the past does not pull down on the neck like Coleridge's albatross, enfold you like a shroud.

First impressions, undoubtedly ungrateful and probably unjust. My rancor is as likely caused by my inability to get a single public telephone to work.

All the same, it is not the Italy I have remembered.

Le Petit Monsieur Triste. Again. That piano, that bass. Why is music, listened to alone in the quiet of night, sometimes so heart-wrenchingly beautiful? It doesn't matter where.

Countless nights when I was thirteen and fourteen and fifteen, surrounded by Spanish bullfight posters in the bar left in the cellar by the GIs billeted in the house in Medway Road during The War, where my father had rigged up an extension speaker from the gramophone upstairs. I learned to ignore the cold, cherishing my solitude too much for it to matter. Beethoven's Eroica, Tchaikovsky's Romeo and Juliet, tears pricking my eyes as the lovers enter, over and over again. So What, Freddie Freeloader, All Blues, Blue in Green, Flamenco Sketches. I bought Kind of Blue in a flea-market in Maidstone, and it was a revelation.

Bob Dylan, inevitably. When the mood took me, Mum's Frank Sinatra, bending those notes so flat, so blue. Stormy weather—Frank sits alone at a bar, staring moodily into a glass of whiskey, cigarette in hand. No one cares.

So *fucking* European. Cortona, Italy, 2001.

The first single I ever bought was the Supremes' Where Did Our Love Go?, the first EP was the Rolling Stones' Five by Five. I spent half my first pay packet from the Strood barge yard where I worked the summer I was fifteen on Blonde on Blonde. The next week I got fired for fighting. Steppenwolf's Born to Be Wild, recorded from the radio, plays on a boxy old reel-to-reel that sits on the floor of the white-walled bedroom where I write poetry on a marble-topped desk. Genèvre, my most treasured effort was called, a love letter to an imaginary but definitely foreign woman in Beat typographics which I picked out with two fingers on an ancient upright Remington.

A room for the summer a few years later in a slum flat on Kingsland Road in Dalston in the East End of London. Traffic pounding past the window day and night, a perpetually unmade bed with dirty sheets, unwashed dishes piling up in the sink—my father was appalled. *New York Is Now!* Ornette Coleman sounded wonderful on the marijuana with which I began the day, the long plaintive wails of his saxophone suspended forever in the midday sunshine. I have the recording with me now, here in Cortona. It sounds just as good without the grass.

It occurs to me that music anchors me.

TUSCANY, ANOTHER HOME FROM HOME. Keats, Shelley, a room with a timeless terracotta view. Standing at the stove in Medway Road with a wooden spoon melting mousetrap cheddar into a saucepan containing among other cacophonies a couple of fresh bay leaves from the tree in Dorothy Phillips's front garden three doors down, aged cloves of garlic from the Indian grocery which was the only place in the Medway Towns you could buy such things, a small tin of tomato puree and a large dash of Worcestershire sauce. I once proudly made my spaghetti for Nanny and Grandad in their house in Sittingbourne, then spoiled it all by dumping the pasta straight in their soup plates without draining it. They gamely ate it up, every last watery strand.

It was at a party at the Phillipses that I had *my first kiss!* The younger sister Julia was my age, thirteen, so pretty in her miniskirt. But it was skinny bespectacled fifteen-year-old Kate who grinned, planted herself on my lap and her lips on mine, and insinuated her tongue into my mouth. I was stunned at the taste, the feel, the thrill of having another human being inside me. Who could ever forget? So sophisticated the Phillipses, Dorothy flamboyant in her kaftan (*I HATE it when people knock the middle class!*) and her quiet architect husband, Peter I think he was called. They had remodeled the old house beautifully, opening it up to the light.

Not long after that Peter left Dorothy for his secretary. I never saw the sisters again.

The stereo is playing what sounds like Astor Piazzolla, a welcome change from the endless synthesized Europop, which reminds me of my daughter Miranda, and how much I miss her. The first time I was in Italy, I remember, it was Bobby Solo singing Una Lagrima sul Viso. I wasn't much older than Miranda is now. I settle myself down at a corner table and let my mind wander. It takes me back to the last time I was traveling alone like this, nearly five years ago now in the summer of 1997, when I was in Prague tidying up loose ends for The Coasts of Bohemia.

One memory stands out sharp from that journey. It is disconcertingly clear—clear, I think, because in retrospect it has come to crystallize so much, though nothing about that evening struck me as especially memorable at the time. It was somewhere in Southern Bohemia, at the end of a day where I gave up searching in the woods for Tomáš and Blanka's cottage and set off in my rented Škoda for the small town of Mirotice where I wanted to see the birthplace of Mikoláš Aleš, a nineteenth-century Czech artist with whom I had become obsessed. I was later to write about Aleš and his lifelong buddy the novelist Alois Jirásek in Common Knowledge. I still think of it as one of my best pieces of writing—it catches that ghostly interweaving of memory and presence, reaching down across the years, clawing back time, better than anything else I have ever done. I wish now I had not let the CK editors talk me out of my original title, which was Contemporaneities.

The dead never let us rest in peace.

I stopped for the night in a pension on the outskirts of a village whose name I do not recall. The sun was going down as I walked down the hill past a duck pond to the one phone box to call my wife. We hadn't spoken in three or four days, not at all unusual when I was away. She was distraught over the water that had started seeping into the Gibbons basement the day before I left and had not let up since. She was pumping it out with a shop-vac, she said, for hours every day. Uselessly, I told her, you might as well try and sweep back the sea with a broom. It will find its own level, do what you will. *Jako studna,* as Mrs. Hájková kept on saying: like a well. Still, I felt miserably guilty at leaving her behind to cope while I was gallivanting about her homeland.

A familiar feeling, this guilt.

On the way back up the hill my thoughts turned, as they had begun so often to do, elsewhere. To my PhD student. Not lascivious thoughts, not romantic thoughts. I just thought about her. Constantly.

So many hours, alone in the truck, driving the frozen winter land-scapes of Alberta.

> SHADOWS ARE FALLING *and I've been here all day,*
> *it's too hot to sleep and time is running away. ...*

The same nasal whine, the same gift for phrasing Bob Dylan shares with Frank Sinatra who also habitually sang off-key and Billie Holiday who scarcely had a voice either. The same ability to imbue the commonplace with pregnancy, to make the everyday profound. The same voice that snared me at fourteen. The same voice, only now it is teetering on the edge of old age. Not Dark Yet, the darkest, sweetest song on Time Out of Mind—the summer I lay rigid night after night beside one woman while trying not to think of another. The night I repeated over and over The Lord's Prayer in a futile attempt to drive her out of my mind.

Lead us not into temptation. Yes but deliver us from what? The older I get, the more difficult it becomes to draw lines in the sand.

Alone in the family room on the acreage I played that track numbingly loud, four, five, six times over, finding an inexplicable solace in this middle-aged return to tangled roots. *Twenty miles out of town in cold irons bound.* The crashing guitars.

> *Well I've been to London and I've been to gay Paree,*
> *I've followed the river and I got to the sea.*
> *I've been down on the bottom of a whirlpool of lies.*
> *I ain't looking for nothing in anyone's eyes.*

Vertigo. Looking out over the cathedral roof again, facing down my demons.

The dawning started the day Dan died. The exact moment was when my wife put a meal I didn't want to eat in front of me on the table, having just hung up the phone on the one person in the world with whom, in that moment, I wanted to talk.

> *And we are here as on a darkling plain*
> *Swept with confused alarms of struggle and flight,*
> *Where ignorant armies clash by night.*

What is there to fear in a simple acknowledgment of love?

THE THAMES ESTUARY OUT PAST CLIFFE, where I used to ride my bicycle forty years ago, always pushing ever onward—an unforgettable landscape of reeds and mudflats, featureless sky meeting featureless sea where the plovers rise and the curlews cry. Another place for being utterly alone, but not really. The hulks were still visible, rotting in the river. They were all out there lurking in the mists, Magwitch the convict, old Joe Gargery the blacksmith, Mrs. Joe who brought Pip up by hand. The file, the flask of grog, the disappearing pie in the pantry. Tickler, of course. Pip, poor clever spineless Pip. Ungrateful little bugger. Poor fucked-up Estella too, though. Miss Haversham can't have been the easiest of guardians, sitting there in Satis House like Shelob the spider surrounded by the ruins of her wedding feast that never was.

Scary, the company I was keeping.

My colleague Doug Aoki tells me I have a face that belongs on the cover of a romance novel. Mills and Boon, I hope. I once read six of my mother's Mills and Boons in a day, wiling away those endless hours of teenage summer sunbathing naked in the high-walled garden in Medway Road slathered in olive oil. It brought me closer to the ancient Greeks, to Sappho and Seferis, the feel, the smell, the frisson of nudity. I like being naked. I have always enjoyed the feel of the elements on my skin, I don't know why. There is some shrewdness in Doug's observation, though likely not in the way he meant it. I have been fool enough to fancy myself from time to time as Darcy: our undeclared five-year court-ship had enough comedic similarities, and she is Eliza Bennet to the life even if she would rather see herself as Emma. She brings me down to earth quick enough. Where is my Pemberley, where is my Prada? Mr. Rochester would be nearer the mark, getting his beloved Jane only as Thornfield Hall tumbles down in flames, the whole sorry mess squarely his fault. Rochester as rendered whether by Charlotte Bronte or Jean Rhys. Both have their insights, the latter, perhaps, more than the former.

So I guess it has to be my lived-in mug after all. A real Keith Richards, me. Another North Kent boy, close but no cigar, not quite London, New Jersey to New York, always aching for something more. Keith and Mick met on the Dartford train, traveling from Memphis to Chicago.

In The Lord of the Rings, whose landscape was at least as real to me as the confluence of the Thames and the Medway which I knew like the back of my hand, I most often identified with Merry and occasionally

Not for use. Zlatá ulička, Prague, 2003.

with Pippin. Sam was too relentlessly servile (it was my teenage friend Jem Thomas who finally nailed this one), Frodo too remote and somehow colorless. Merry and Pippin were always getting into trouble. I could not see myself as Aragorn or Boromir, let alone as Gandalf; the noble and sensitive Faramir, yes, at a pinch. I would readily have changed places with any of the female characters though, be it brave Eowyn who disguises herself as a boy to go to the war and slays the Nazgul (and falls for Faramir), raven-haired Arwen Evenstar, Elrond's daughter, who gives up her elvish immortality for love of Aragorn—even Galadriel at that moment when she drops her queenly mantle and appears before Frodo as a simple elven woman.

When Aragorn was no more Arwen left Minas Tirith and lay down to die, alone, on a flower-covered hill in Lothlorien. Galadriel and Celeborn had long ago passed over the sea. Only the land remembers them.

Most of all I would have liked to be the elf maiden Luthien Tinuviel, the nightingale, who snared Beren forever when he spied her dancing in a moonlit glade in Doriath. Together they passed through many perils until they wrested the silmaril from the iron crown of Morgoth and Beren was slain at the last by a wolf coming from the gates of Angband.

Odd, isn't it, where the imagination transports us: how far out of—or into—ourselves? I had forgotten this adolescent gender bending, this easy slipping in and out of an ever changing cast of characters.

But Luthien was so beautiful.

Where I lost myself most thoroughly in Tolkien's world was in the scholarly appendices to the book, which root the War of the Ring in a five thousand–year span. Everywhere the past surrounds them, making a crazy sense out of the unfairness of their lives. It holds *all* the keys, at least for the Wise. Frodo did not ask to inherit the Dark Lord's ring. When Sam cooks him the rabbit with herbs (but without any salt) that Gollum has caught in the leafy glades of Ithilien, you catch an echo of Ar-Pharazon the Golden planting his standard on the Undying Lands, the day the world was changed forever, three thousand years before. Frodo pays the price of the pride that wrecked Numenor and brought Elendil the Tall and his two sons Isildur and Anarion back to Middle Earth, fleeing in nine ships with the White Tree and the Seeing Stones.

I shall take this as weregild for my father and brother says Isildur as he cuts the ring from Sauron's hand.

I was entranced by Rosemary Sutcliffe's novels of Roman Britain at an earlier age. My favorite cartoon character was Karl the Viking, a blond-haired captured Saxon boy who grows up to become a Viking warrior in The Lion (or was it The Tiger?), the two comics I got through the post weekly at Dashmonden Close. Can we *remember* what it was like to be a Roman sentry on Hadrian's Wall, far from home, cold and fearful and missing your girl? I thought so, the feeling was so tangible. I still thought so in my teens, reading a lament of exile on the Great Wall of China, possibly by Li Ho, written more than a thousand years ago on the other side of the earth—just to be remembered by me, sitting in a gloomy house in the middle of the Tuscan winter. I think it came from a treasured black Penguin called Poems of the Late T'ang, but I wouldn't swear to it, this many winters on.

The world we pass through—the world that passes through us—is layer upon layer of signifiers that everywhere reach back and beyond us yet penetrate to the core of our being. Why restrict the term *memory* to what one can be said to have personally experienced, when neither the personal nor experience has any meaning, any substance, outside of this matrix? It misses the essence of who we are, eternally cavorting at the perilous intersection of pasts and presents, words and things, dodging the speeding Jaguars and the runaway trucks.

I was with the Philippine armies at the battle of Reykjavik says Dr. Who to Marcus Griel, the butcher of Brisbane, as he time-travels the universe in a cranky blue Victorian police box. The year was 5006 or thereabouts.

Aragorn tells the tale of Luthien Tinuviel to the hobbits six nights out from Bree under Weathertop, trying to keep the darkness at bay as the Black Riders close in. However dark it was that night, it was a still darker place, the First Age in which Luthien and Beren lived. Tolkien provided few and tantalizing glimpses of that epic time, just enough to make me long to read the Silmarillion on which he was rumored to be working. Its posthumous publication, when I was a PhD student in Durham, was one of the disappointments of my life. So dry, so pedantic, just strings of words on a page. That may say much more about me then than it does about Tolkien. Recently I reread the book, with immense pleasure, recapturing at least an echo of the times and places it would have transported me had I been able to read it at thirteen.

A tightrope, writing.

I am half afraid to see the film of The Lord of the Rings they are making now in New Zealand, though the landscapes there would be perfect for Middle Earth. Those trackless hills outside Wellington on the way to Ali and Sue's, bleak and wild and swathed in mists. The desert road by the three volcanoes.

My fear is that it will not match up to what I remember.

I WENT TO SCHOOL, NEVERTHELESS, IN SATIS HOUSE. This is not just meta-phor. I really did. That is what it was called, the white Georgian mansion opposite Rochester Castle in which I did my sixth-form studies—the French Revolution and the Roman Republic, Tess and Jude, Chaucer and Milton, Antony and Cleopatra and The Winter's Tale.

The soldier's pole is fallen, and there is nothing left remarkable beneath the visiting moon.

My salad days. When we tripped the light fantastic, left our virginities on the coast.

By the time I reached the sixth form my body had been school ruled and crocodile filed, blancoed and boatered, paraded and inspected, chapeled and cricketed, ruggered and rattaned, into—well into what, exactly? Certainly not that docile body my students so glibly prattle on about, parroting Foucault but never talking about bodies at all. Foucault himself learned much from the bath houses, where few of his acolytes ever stray. Not least that disciplines, academic and otherwise, can be pleasurable.

Mine was a *disciplined* body, for sure. A body to which much has been done, and with which much can therefore be ventured. A body that is quite comfortable with being seen, whether dressed or naked. Above all, a body that is *known*—a body in and with which one is completely at home.

Atten—SHUN! Stand aaaaat—EASE!

For a prefect's beating, which was very much more to be feared than anything dished out by the masters, we had first to change into flimsy gym shorts. For years you watch them, the prefects, lounging on the school steps, one elegant hand in the pocket, lords of all they survey. For years you watch them while they are watching you, and you learn. Ease, grace, nonchalance. A hint of disdain. A sublime confidence that you will let nothing in the world throw you off your stride, a *fuck you* to fate.

If you can keep your head when all about you ... The undying gayness of the English public school boy, which has precious little to do with who you fuck.

Staaaand—EASY!

Oh yes, I loved it.

Whether Dickens took the name from the existing house, or the house was renamed from the novel (but why on earth should anyone want to

Diverted traffic. Mayfair, London, 2002.

do *that?*), I don't know. *Satis*—enough, in Latin, if my memory serves me right. As in (I Can't Get No) Satisfaction. Anyway it cannot have been coincidental, the name. This was Dickens country through and through. The Mystery of Edwin Drood, Dickens's unfinished last novel, is set in and around Rochester Cathedral, where I was seduced but not touched, or maybe I was touched but not seduced, by Rusty Willard at age ten, and his details are exact. The great writer lived a few miles up the London Road at Gad's Hill near Cobham, and obviously knew the district well.

What do you get when you play a country song backwards?

Your dog back, your truck back, your life back.

THE SMELL OF CARBOLIC SOAP and the sight of bare bums in the showers after games, wet leaves on autumn pavements, the marvels of marbles and glossy brown conkers. *Amo, amas, amat, amamus, amatis, amant, roll me over in the clover roll me over lay me down and do it again.*

I trudged back from school in the drizzly winter dark up the long drag of Frindsbury Hill, having spent my bus fare on a sixpenny bag of chips dredged in salt and drenched in malt vinegar. If I permitted myself just ONE chip each time I passed another lamppost they would last me to the top. *Half past one, the street lamp muttered.* In summertime I varied the route. Up the steep narrow path between the two long-abandoned chalk quarries to Frindsbury Church, through the churchyard and across the Upnor Road where Jon Cooper skidded the Mark Ten a few years later with me inside it, a quick foray into the strawberry field, then home. Nobody was much bothered which way I came home so long as I wasn't too late. I was given unbelievable freedom to wander as a kid. We would all eat the strawberries for tea.

If instead of heading up to Frindsbury Church you kept to the riverbank, going toward Upnor, you would eventually hit a narrow path along a crumbling cliff face that led to the cave. It wasn't much of a cave: a high shallow cavern, open to the river, scooped out of the dried mud. Fifty yards further along I discovered another cave. The entrance was a mere hole in the ground, dark and uninviting. We came back the next day and explored it with stolen matches and candles, me and Durrrk and others whose names I have forgotten. I was the first to crawl down the tunnel, maybe twenty feet in, to a chamber where it was possible to stand: it was five feet high, perhaps. I was far from oblivious to the mountain of earth above me, but refused to let it intimidate me, daring the rest of them to follow.

I could feel Dad tensing as we took the path along the eroded cliff face; I treated it as an opportunity to show off my nimbleness. *Like a mountain goat,* I remember thinking, some cliché from some book as ever skipping into my mind. He looked doubtful as I showed him the first cave, but not too much so. The second cave, the one I discovered, was a different matter. He didn't shout. He didn't swear.

I don't want you to come here ever again, do you hear me? Do you understand me? EVER! He was trembling like a leaf in the wind. God if he had seen me that day on the cathedral roof.

It must have been around this time—maybe a year or two earlier. I won't go so far as to call it *the calamity,* but it has certainly stuck in my mind.

R. LEEKS they read, the letters scratched into my handsome brown leather satchel, probably with a penknife. *Thief!* some other kid hissed, and they all took up the refrain, *Thief! Thief! Thief!* It was in the Paddock, near the Cricket Pavilion, by St. Margaret's House where the boarders lived, the same grassy bank where three or four years later Brian Gilbert read me Keats's Ode to Autumn. I told them the satchel was given to me by my Auntie Louie and used to belong to my cousin Bobby.

Oh yeah, if he's your cousin how come he has a different name from you, huh? someone sneered. I asked him whether *his* cousins all had the same surname as him, but so far as they were concerned it was a clinching argument. I was just trying to be clever, as usual.

Thief! Thief! Thief! they continued to chant. I didn't have the words, or likely the knowledge of family relationships, to explain to them that Auntie Louie was my father's sister, who had changed her name when she married blind Robert Leeks, after whom my older cousin Bobby was named.

They wouldn't have listened anyway. It had been going on for weeks.

I didn't cry, when Mr. Jameson caned me. That came afterwards, in the playground, when the boys gathered round me in a circle for the first time, doctor's sons, farmer's sons, shouting *Thief! Thief! Thief!*

I wasn't stealing, I protested, I was SCRUMPING.

I would never *steal* a single strawberry from a fruiterer's display, but slipping into an unguarded field or orchard was different. But I was quite unable to explain this distinction to my fellow-pupils, who did not live on housing estates and who had not gone to County Primary schools, though it was clear as the light of day to me. Not that I had ever given it any thought. There had never been any need. An early lesson in the embeddedness of language games in forms of life, not to mention the slipperiness of the signifier, but I hadn't read Wittgenstein or Derrida then and nor had they.

No, this is not a prelude to yet another whine about the evils of the English class system, the pitiful inbetweenness of the poor scholarship boy. I got a damned good education at King's and I am grateful for it. I have seldom been lost for words since. They kept their distance after I got an arm-lock on Peter Evett's throat and half-choked him one morning recess, rolling over and over and over in the muddy grass on the Paddock. It felt good.

Fight! Fight! Fight! they were chanting this time.

As for the cane, the fearsome rattan, I made that my very own too, in spades. I'm not scared of *you*.

Bobby is dead now. *Years ago. At 37. Cancer.* So Mum told me at the fag-end of last fall, in the cold and damp beginnings of a New Zealand spring.

THE TRAIN TO TEDDINGTON STOPS at every station, a thirty-five-minute journey. It is a ten-minute walk down the High Street. I have never been here before. Sunday, and the shops are closed. The streets are empty. All the way I do what I seldom do, think about my father.

We spent much of my teenage years fighting and then kept our resentful distance. The last time we had much to do with one another was when I tried to persuade him to give Mum a half-way decent divorce settlement when she was penniless in Melbourne after splitting up with the Australian flying doctor for whom she abandoned Dad, and we fought again. That was fifteen years ago now, when I was still in Glasgow.

It is not a matter of the memories flooding back this time, because these are things I never allowed myself to forget. I nursed them.

The morning when I was ten or eleven when out of nowhere he started yelling at me, making me clean my shoes over and over again, *knowing* I would miss the bus and be late for school. I despised him: he knew full well that I would be punished, and not by him. The barely concealed satisfaction, or so it seemed to me, when he told me he had found me the job in Hastings after I was suspended from school. How on earth was I to study for the A Levels, get to university, if I was to spend all day laboring on a building site? The parental contribution he seldom made to my grant when I was a student, the many promised checks that never arrived on time. His gleeful prediction, leaning half-pissed over the bar of a London pub, the week before I sat my finals: *You'll just miss your First, won't you boy?* Him sitting silent in the kitchen of my first marital home in Eccles Road in Battersea, never troubling to remove his coat. His niggardly reaction when I told him of Natasha's

Vanitas. Aix-en-Provence, France, 2002.

birth many years later: no congratulations, just a curt *I thought she couldn't have any.*

I invited him up to Glasgow to see his first grandchild, a symbolic burying of the hatchet. He never came.

During a blazing row between my parents when I was sixteen I threatened to drop him cold if he didn't lay off Mum, who was in tears. He drew himself up, thought twice of it, and stormed off to the Marquis of Lorne slamming the front door behind him. After everyone was in bed I packed a bag—mainly with books—and ran away from home, hitchhiking through the Dartford Tunnel to Essex University where my friend Jem was in his first year.

I left a note for my mother on the kitchen table:
Take the kids and leave the bastard.

THAT'S HOW I HAVE REMEMBERED IT. But what I actually left for my mother on the table was this:

Message
I have taken his jacket.
It will be cold.
Colder for you, in his bed.
I have left you a chance.
Take the other two—
He will be colder, alone.

He kept it. I stumbled across it among his things in the house in Burnham, after he was dead. Another found object, full of Proustian disorientations.

Charing Cross through Waterloo and London Bridge to Dartford, Gravesend and the Medway Towns, then on past Sittingbourne and Faversham to the sea. After Gravesend—round about the village of Higham, I think, where Mickey Chance lived—the tracks disappear under the chalk hills of the North Downs. Darkness, a rush of wind, the smell of smoke, the amplified rattling of the carriages—then all at once a flood of light. Elderberries, banks of stinging nettles, flowers that flourish in railway cuttings. Morning glory. The tunnel closes in again almost before the moment has had time to register. When the train finally re-emerges by the river below Frindsbury Church at Strood, you are in another world.

Looming landmarks in a small landscape, in the plateaus of the week, in the passages of adolescence—Rochester Gaumont where I saw Pete Townshend smash guitars on stage before The Who released My Generation, the fleapit in Rainham with the double seats in the back two rows where I never got to take a girl. The Gillingham cinema whose name and location I no longer remember where I watched Zorba the Greek and The Ipcress File, the smoke from Peter Stuyvesants—the foreignness of the name attracted me—curling languorously upward from the corner of my mouth. I hadn't yet learned to inhale. I sucked Polo Mints and trailed my fingers along walls on the walk home, hoping the brick would act like pumice stone.

She was thirteen, I was fourteen—my first girlfriend. She let me reach inside her bra and touch her breast. I don't recall which cinema, what movie. I remember her name, Mandy, and her smell. I remember nothing else about her. As so often, our memories are snapped from their surroundings as if by a zoom lens.

The Medway Folk Club, Wednesday nights in the room above the pub by Rochester Bridge, three pints of bitter and a woozy ride home. Mum took me to hear Arlo Guthrie who sang Alice's Restaurant there, and Tom Paxton, and Ramblin' Jack Elliot, legends all. One time Hughie the docker, our very own little red-faced Hughie the docker, varied his usual repertoire of Irish rebel songs with a stirring rendition of The Sash My Father Wore. He apologized to all for the ecumenical lapse, but it was, he said, a fine old tune.

It is old but it is beautiful, its colors they are fine.

1690—spray-painted on a slum wall in Glasgow, three centuries after King Billy thrashed the Papists at the Battle of the Boyne. Memories like curses, digging up old grudges like dogs' bones.

My mother brought Hughie home once. My father, as was the custom in our house whenever Mum's friends visited, was unbelievably surly.

Why does this recollection of Hughie singing The Sash lead me to a church in Manhattan, where Paul Sweezy took me to hear Pete Seeger in a benefit for (I think) Nicaragua? Probably in 1978, on my first visit to New York, but possibly a few years later. I forget now exactly when it was that the Sandinistas took up residence in British universities, though I do remember an unaccustomed feeling of ridiculousness—it was around the time of the visit to New Lanark—in Nigel Haworth's flat in Glasgow. I suddenly realized that I had not the slightest interest in Nicaragua, the topic of the conversation that was flowing as freely as the wine, a conversation that eventually encircled the globe.

Bright eyes sparkled on the women in the candlelight.

Harvie Ramsay must have been there that night, big slow amiable Harvie with the size thirteen feet who loved Monty Python and Dr. Who, my co-author, with Philip Corrigan, of two books it would be as troubling, now, to own up to as to repudiate. Harvie died suddenly earlier this summer. It came as a shock. I can't honestly say I mourn him, we were never that close and hadn't been in touch in fifteen years. Happily married, as they say, at the time, I dutifully distanced myself after Harvie scandalously left his wife for his student. It is a trifle late to say I have since got my comeuppance.

What I mourn is another piece of the jigsaw snatched away while I am still around to remember it.

Prematurely snatched away, it seems—but I begin to wonder. After all it began with Nanny in Saint Bart's Hospital above the Medway where Mum worked in the path lab later with Frank Spenser who showed me his pornographic drawings and took me to hear Danny Abse reading his poetry to jazz. Screens round the bed, tubes coming out of her nose. She couldn't speak. She squeezed my hand. I couldn't cry then either, though everyone else in the house did, not even when the coffin slid away behind the curtains at the crematorium and Grandad's legs buckled under him, just like that.

It continued with Mickey Chance and Jon Cooper, Philip Abrams and Kirsty Larner. Kirsty, whom those of us who liked her affectionately knew as The Devil, bought herself a motorbike the day after the reappearance of her cancer was confirmed. She went out a few months later to the strains of the Old Grey Men, as she used to call them (it would be wrong here to spell it in the American fashion), raising the rafters of Glasgow University chapel with a rousing chorus of *Who would true Valour see, Let her come hither.* Kirsty orchestrated her own funeral service a few days before she died, adapting Bunyan less out of feminist conviction than sheer glee at the side-splitting image. She left four hundred pounds in her will, to be spent on single malts for the wake. I drank Highland Park in her memory, and got guttered.

Then Dan.

Above Saint Bart's there is a park. In that park there is a bench. On that bench Marian and I spent many hours kissing in the cold some four years later, shyly exploring what was under one another's clothes. Marian used to come with me sometimes to the Folk Club, but her heart was in Vladimir Ashkenazy playing Beethoven. We graduated to lying in bed together naked, but did no more than touch. It was, I think, the last innocent relationship of my life, unburdened by futures or pasts.

Seeger sang his anthems, probably Plane Crash at Los Gatos, certainly Guantanamera and The Marching Song of the Red Army. The church was half-empty, the audience elderly even then. I thought about how thirty years earlier the white-haired man beside me had started up a Marxist magazine, Monthly Review, in the depths of the Cold War. Sweezy was the only one who had the guts and the gall to refuse both Senator Joe McCarthy's bullying questions and the pyrrhic safety of the Fifth Amendment.

Are you or have you ever been?

Paul Sweezy was Westchester to the core.

Goodbye to my Juan, goodbye Rosalita
Adios mi amigo; Jesus y Maria
You won't have a name when you ride the big airplane
All they will call you, will be deportee.

Another hall somewhere in the Medway Towns, in Chatham this time I think, another benefit for another good cause. A nervous girl my own age on the podium, pretty with puppy fat and long brown hippie hair and a guitar. She definitely did sing Plane Crash at Los Gatos, and she had the most luscious voice I had ever heard. It was a voice you could see, and touch, and taste, and smell, a rich, dark chocolate mezzo-soprano. Incredibly, she agreed to go out with me.

Her name was Kate McLean.

The year was 1968, between school and university. Students were rioting in the streets of Paris, tearing up the paving stones in search of the beach.

Hughie, it dawned on me later, was a mascot for the small-town intelligentsia of teachers and librarians and lab technicians who frequented the Medway Folk Club, the only one among us who was—that ultimate object of English desire—actually *working class.* Such places cry out for a Chekhov to anatomize their longings. I affected Spanish workmen's boots with *ANARCHY* painted across the toes and my father's threadbare donkey jacket—*his jacket,* the one I took the night I ran away from home—and was working hard on my glottal stops.

I have since come to dislike folk music intensely, to distrust anything that pretends to authenticity.

KATE, I HAVE SINCE BEEN REMINDED, was with me that summer, the summer of 1968, on the trip to Amsterdam.

I woke up around midnight on a wooden bench in Ostend harbor bereft of baggage, wallet, passport, and any memory of how I entered the country. I had gotten hopelessly drunk on the crossing, on, I think, Martini. The strange thing is that I can *now* recollect, with absolute clarity, the gentle sway of the boat, the warm light of the afternoon sun on the sea diffusing in a genial alcoholic haze.

Later Kate told me she had steered me through the Belgian customs, persuading them I was seasick, and taken the wallet and passport for safekeeping when I lapsed from incoherence into stupor. We hitchhiked to Amsterdam the next day where we met an Italian student named Michele in Dam Square. We got on wonderfully, undeterred by the fact that the nearest we had to a shared language was half-forgotten Latin. We (of course) invited him back to England, heedless of requirements for visas, return tickets, and sufficient funds to support his stay in the United Kingdom. Europe and the Chunnel lay far in the future. Dover was closer then to Durban than to Calais.

My parents received a telephone call from the Dover police informing them that their son was being detained while trying to import an alien.

I visited Michele, who lived with his parents in the run-down flats of the Olympic Village in Rome, during the spring break of the following year. I bought a large volume of Gramsci's Scritti Politici there, of which I was inordinately proud and quite unable to read a word. On the way back, as a favor to Kate's elder sister Alison—who was now living with boyfriend and baby in a commune in Copenhagen—I picked up a package she had left in Paris and wanted taken home. This time Her Majesty's Customs wanted to know what I was doing with a box of purple knickers.

The story holds little interest, apart maybe from the color purple. Except for this. Why, when I began this memoir with the smell of tobacco in the Amsterdam mists, a memory every bit as capable of bringing the past flooding back as the taste of Proust's madeleine, did I recollect myself alone, as a solitary Jack Kerouac wannabe? It took Mum, entertaining us with the tale of her frantic drive to Dover, to bring any of this to mind at all.

The kiss. Mayfair, London, 2001.

Where, in and out of my memory, did that girl go, who obsessed me day and night for well over a year? Dad, of course, used to delight in mimicking her *plummy* accent.

I WALK THE LENGTH of the Grace Anderson Ward. His is the last bed on the right. He is sitting on the bed dressed in flannel pants and cardigan with his reading glasses on, doing a crossword. He looks better than I expected, if painfully thin. He always did have legs like matchsticks. It is the same pinched intelligent face, the same luxuriant head of hair that is gray now but nowhere near white. He wears it, as he always did, slightly too long: a vanity we share.

I am momentarily thrown by the English crookedness of his teeth, which I had either never noticed as odd or long ago forgotten.

It has, after all, been fifteen years.

He doesn't recognize me at first. I tell him who I am. *Derek? Derek! What are YOU doing here? Delighted to see you mate!* He shakes my hand, *Ow not so bloody hard!* he winces. He repeats it again and again throughout the three and a half hours I spend with him, *Delighted to see you mate!* He has evidently forgotten that I am going through a divorce, and thinks Neil is in Australia. He is hazy about my age *(Fifty? Good God are you that old! You certainly wear it well!),* uncertain about the number of my children. He complains about losing his memory, especially of the sequence of events that brought him here. *I lost it, boy, I just lost it.*

Watching the other patients he fears for himself. *Christ I don't want to get like that. I'd rather die right now.* He's obviously getting old. But he's sharp as nails. The malicious humor, that so often had us in stitches, is still there.

I'm an unsociable old sod, he tells me by way of explanation of the weeks that passed before Alison found him in the Burnham house suffering from malnutrition and hypothermia, weeks in which he had told her again and again on the telephone to *Fuck off!*

You always were, I say.

I'm getting a bit deaf, he responds. *Did you say "Me too"?*

I laugh. Don't worry about my kids, he says. They'll come back when they want something. *Hi Dad, remember me?*

I get the double entendre, as I am intended to. That sardonic smile; I have it too. He is still sparring with me after all these years, testing my mettle, just like he always did. He passes me the paper. *Can you help me out? I've done most of it.* It is today's Daily Telegraph cryptic crossword, and he has filled in all but two answers.

He knows damned well that I can't. I never could.

Mum chucked the packed lunch she had just made for me, parceled up in the usual Sunblest bread wrapper, full force across the kitchen, catching Dad on the side of the face. Tomato and egg everywhere. We all thought it was hilarious afterwards.

You want memories?

There were the times he took me with him as a child to the hotels and pubs he designed, to Muddeford in Hampshire, to Aldeburgh, to York— he passed the long train ride down to Devon with the Telegraph crossword while I jabbered on incessantly, excited by the new worlds passing by outside the window. He made the time to climb Hay Tor with me, puffing and panting up the rocky hill. His hand under my tummy or my chin in the icy sea at Seaford, telling me to relax and let the water bear me. The matchbox tops he carefully saved for me from all around the world, scrounging them from everyone he met. The four-drawer document cabinet he brought home from work one day, spending hours in the shed measuring and sawing strips of wood, gluing them firmly in place so I would have a fitting housing for my collection of minerals and rocks. I won first prize in the school hobbies exhibition for that, two years running.

The wall unit he constructed for me in my bedroom in Dashmonden Close out of odds and sods, delighting in his craft. The way he divided the room later with a wardrobe, a chest of drawers, and a Venetian blind, sensing that I was getting old enough to need some privacy from my younger brother. I had already watched Neil nearly die in that room from complications of the measles. Mum in tears, again. The rockeries and rustic arches, the crazy-paving paths and honeysuckle trellises he built for Mum's relentless gardens. The ridiculous cottage he made out of my cool white bedroom in Medway Road when I went to university and Alison inherited it, suspending wattle panels from the ceiling. So often cruel and sarcastic with words, he could be marvelously kind with his hands.

The night he got drunk with his mates after work and called up the BBC, demanding to speak with the literary editor, belligerently inform- ing him that *his* boy wrote poetry that could knock the rubbish they were broadcasting into a cocked hat. The times in my teens he would say *Fancy a pint?* and take me out and thrash me at bar billiards in the Marquis. Oddly enough we were probably closer then, when we were going at each other hammer and tongs, than at any time in our lives before or since. *Don't talk to me about the bloody working class, I have to deal with the buggers every day.*

One of Dad's colleagues took me aside at the party my parents threw in the bar in the cellar in Medway Road to celebrate the marriage they had never wanted. I was just twenty-one, and knew better than them in this like I did in everything else. *It was the saddest day of my life,* Mum told me last year. I don't remember the man's name: another of the work hard play hard building contractors with Yorkshire accents and gold taps in their bathrooms that Mum so hated, holding them personally respon- sible for all her unfulfilled dreams.

I know your father gives you a hard time, he told me, bleary, sentimen- tal, half-cut, drooling in his beer. *But he loves you, Derek. You wouldn't believe how proud of you he is. He never shuts up about his clever young son.*

Here above all I do not trust my memories. Some I have collated and narrated so often that they have long lost touch with whatever gave rise to them, circling round and round each other in a prison yard of their own. With others, I have been remarkably careless.

Silly old cunt. Who am I, of all people, to pass judgment?

I get up to go, leaving the three books of Daily Telegraph Cryptic Crosswords I have brought for him lying on the bed.

WE ALL MADE THE FUNERAL, a year and a half later. It was the first time we had all been together in nearly thirty years, Mum, Dad, me, Alison, Neil. *Of course he never liked you,* Mum let slip one night when we were sitting round the table in Alison's kitchen, the way that mothers like to do. *Thought you were a bit of a pansy.* Things hanging half unsaid, things unsayable, too many things said by half.

The strains of The Seekers' The Carnival is Over overwhelmed the little chapel at the crematorium, irresistibly recalling Judith Durham's great big tits.

LBJ, LBJ, HOW MANY KIDS have you killed today?

George Gilbert, yes yet another Gilbert, the schoolteacher who lived up the road just down from the Marquis of Lorne, opposite the cricket ground where occasionally you could catch a county match. My mother, who knew George from the Folk Club, didn't trust him, but I spent many hours in his basement kitchen getting an education in communist ways. I can date it, I think, quite precisely. My friend Jem Thomas went to university a year before me, in the fall of 1967. At that time we were both styling ourselves Anarchists. It was Jem, the first grammar school boy I knew, who introduced me to Kropotkin, Bakunin, Malatesta, names every bit as poetic as any in The Lord of the Rings. But by the time he came home that Christmas, I had a confession to make.

I was a *Marxist.*

Fortuitously Jem, too, had fallen under the old wizard's spell at Essex: how could any intelligent boy then not? It was in the air. We sat up in my bedroom in Medway Road, too excited by our revolutionary discovery to sleep, talking dialectics and making collages the whole night through. That odd tenderness between males—I have seldom felt it since. Once inseparable, Jem and I drifted apart after he fell in love with Sue, who later, a child later, in turn divorced him.

In retrospect, that night was the swansong of a friendship; which is why, probably, I remember it quite as clearly as I do.

It was George Gilbert who had been responsible for my conversion to Marxism, talking with me first at the bus stop (*Oh yes?* he asked, actually seeming interested, which adults usually were not, when I proudly informed him I was an Anarchist), posing questions I couldn't begin to answer, then lending me books I might find interesting. The Communist Manifesto, Wages, Price and Profit, eventually (*Keep it, son, I don't need it any more*) volume 1 of Capital.

Those wonderful rolling Victorian cadences.

George opened the door not just to ideas but to a history and a culture hitherto utterly unknown to me, cradled as I had been in my public school. I remain grateful to him. It was there quite as much in the air in his kitchen, thick with the smoke of the pipe on which he was always thoughtfully sucking, the endless cups of tea his wife had forever on the boil, the queer assortment of people, *real* people, *workers,* who were constantly popping in and out, and their talk of the whole wide world, as it was in anything that George actually said. I do remember him telling me though of his experiences as an education officer on troop ships during The War, when he took full advantage of the alliance with Uncle Joe to hijack every lecture for agitprop.

And when the boys came home, the first thing they did was to boot out Churchill.

He chuckled. I learned the names Gallipoli, Tonypandy—talismans of a knowledge others did not possess.

It was in the spring of the following year, after I had finished what turned out to be a very short stint laboring in Hastings, that I started dating Kate. Her father Tony, an extramural lecturer for Kent University whose socialist pedigree was at least as impeccable as George Gilbert's own—he was of that Oxbridge generation of Philby, Burgess and Maclean, and Anthony Blunt—expanded my horizons still further. *Was* he in Spain? (Hemingway, Orwell, Auden, Spender, Poetry of the 1930s, another treasured Penguin.) I think so, even though his scholarly fuffiness belied it.

It was in Kate's house that I ate green peppers for the first time, stuffed with rice, and learned what a vinaigrette was, neither salad cream nor sugared water. The world was opening up to me by the day. I couldn't wait to be part of it all. America was burning, Paris was burning, the tide was turning in Vietnam.

One day there was just George and his wife there, in the kitchen. Something felt wrong, terribly wrong, almost as if somebody had died. Slowly, haltingly, angrily, George told me he had turned in his party card. The occasion was something to do with the Soviet Union and the colonels' junta in Greece, whether it was diplomatic recognition or the signing of a trade pact I can no longer recall. But I can remember being puzzled.

Why *Greece?*

It seemed a trivial reason, almost as if he had been waiting for an excuse to jump ship. George had remained in the party, after all, in 1956, after Hungary, when so many had left, and given me plausible reasons why. For a communist of his generation Greece held many memories—a lost civil war, what emerged much later as a betrayal at Yalta. Churchill again. But still.

Over the next few weeks I watched him slowly fall apart. It was unutterably sad. Nobody came to the house any more. The party had been the pivot around which his life revolved. It wasn't the same, his kitchen, and nor was he. The heart had gone out of them both. Soon I stopped dropping in too, putting my head down and hurrying on by.

Very much later, I have no idea when, I began to wonder just how long George had been going through the motions, and at what point, and why, the mask became just too uncomfortable to wear any longer—whatever the personal price.

How *do* you handle betrayals?

THE SUN COMES OUT and it is all at once as it was supposed to be. Down a dark alleyway, round a corner, and there is a sudden intensity of light, light everywhere, striping the sides of the buildings, suffusing the courtyards and squares, sharp-angled shadows on the walls. Far above, thin slices of bright blue sky, pure and clean as a Mondrian painting. Colors on shutters and stucco, sun-bleached and subtle, boxes of fruit and vegetables gay outside the opened stores, oranges and purples and greens. The old stones glow.

The door of the thirteenth-century town hall, up the broad steps from the Piazza della Repubblica, is framed by two matching white marble tablets. One, erected on December 16, 1945, lists the names of partisans from the Commune di Cortona who gave their lives *pro patria* in The War that had just ended, *vittime della furiosa Teutonica*. The other, which was added forty years later on December 4, 1984, remembers those townsfolk whose valor gained them military decorations as they too fell pro patria, four of the twenty-three in World War I, the other nineteen fighting on the side of the Axis between 1939 and 1943.

Irony? Or is it just that whatever we cannot forget we must in the end forgive—if, that is, we are to go on at all?

Little shrines everywhere, niches in the wall where people leave flowers and potted plants. Who and what are they remembering? The peal of church bells, the smell of wood-smoke hanging in the streets. Someone is practicing a trumpet, up and down the scales, up and down, down and up, over and over again. So European, and so familiar. I no longer feel that claustrophobia I did when I first arrived. I know I could melt into this place as I once did into Durham or Prague, with just the occasional hankering for the billboards that line the Calgary Trail, the wide open Alberta skies. Love is not incompatible with absence—or so I tell myself, anyway.

I take my evening stroll down the Via Nazionale, watching the groups of men who gather in the streets before dinner to talk and smoke. Not feeling like cooking for one I stop at a taverna, order a dish of spaghetti with truffles, linger over a half-liter of red while I wait for her to call me on my new telefonino. I think about the recent e-mails she has passed on from Neil.

And thanks most importantly for urging the Prof once again into contact with family, he writes.

Family matters. His marriage is falling apart.

I get irrationally fearful, sometimes, that we will break up *because* Mum broke up with her Australian doctor two years after she left Dad. I shall never forget Mum the night before she went. I flew down to London from Glasgow to wish her bon voyage. We met in a restaurant on or near Charlotte Street, possibly Milou's where I used often to go in the late 1970s and early 1980s with Philip. But possibly not. Milou's is long gone. What *I* remember from that night is a woman deeply, ecstatically in love. She looked like a young girl again. She looked like I had always wanted to remember her. What *she* remembers is no more than a convenient crutch, or so she told me last fall on the long drive back to Kerikeri from Cape Rianga.

He gave me the courage I needed to leave your father, that's all.
That's all?

Whereof we cannot speak thereof we must be silent.

Apparently the old boy didn't know who you were. Thought you were a friend of mine, Neil's e-mail continued.

Snow on palms. Cortona, 2001.

My heart momentarily faltered when I read it. It would be poetic justice of a sort. Alison reassures me, though, that the first thing Dad told her when she arrived back from Christmas with Mum in New Zealand to take him home from the Teddington hospital was that I had stopped off on my way from Canada to Italy to see him, and he hasn't shut up about my visit since.

Nice, isn't it, to be remembered?

The pasta arrives. I still haven't made up my mind about truffles. The voluptuousness of the aroma both seduces and repels me, like the undulations of the waitress's ass.

> ***Damien Hirst*** | My first question, OK?
> *Dazed & Confused* | Go on then.
> What are you afraid of?
> **Difficult question. Nothing really. ...**
> Do you know what I'm afraid of?
> **What?**
> First of all, my girlfriend leaving me, then maybe death, after that, nothing.

The past is always tense, she says, delighting in her pun. It was always her mind, her quicksilver mind. But those tiny breasts, the barest hint of a womanly swell. The slenderness of her wrists. The blackness of her hair on her skin as she sleeps, the way the summer sun makes her face glow gold. The curve of her abdomen, the gentle hillocks of her behind.

I've never said this to anybody, she told me after the awards ceremony where I was still, ludicrously, her supervisor, and she my stellar student. Sitting in the parking lot in the cab of my truck, our five-year dance around Wittgenstein finally done. *I'm yours.*

> *And when the angels ask me to recall*
> *the thrill of them all,*
> *then I shall tell them I remember you.*

Frank Ifield, a fragment from a pop song of my youth.

A NAKED WOMAN STANDS ON TIPTOES by a sideboard. The meager light from the window illuminates only her shoulders and her derrière: think Edward Hopper noir. Behind her is the horn of an antique phonograph. On the sideboard stands a long-playing record I used once to own, Lotte Lehmann singing Schumann Lieder.

Tension upon My Toes, China Hamilton calls his photograph. It recalls a second-hand store specializing in historic operatic recordings behind Waterloo Station in London, run by a garrulous old queen with a formidable knowledge of the history of singing. Roger, his name was. One day I bought an old record album by Lotte Lehmann from him called *Songs of Vienna*, containing the Richard Tauber warhorse *Wien, Wien, nür Du allein* and similar mitteleuropische sentimentalities, sickly-sweet as Sachertorte.

I made some remark about kitsch. He rounded on me.

Look at the date and place of recording, he said.

New York, 1940 or '41.

And?

And I remembered: Lehmann was part-Jewish. One of the greatest Wagner singers of the twentieth century, she fled Vienna and Europe shortly after recording what is probably the most incandescent rendition of Act I of Die Walküre ever committed to disk, under the baton of Bruno Walter, another Jew, in 1938. Her beloved Vienna.

After The War, she could never bear to go back.

He nodded, satisfied that I understood what I was purchasing. *Some of the saddest records ever made.*

The signs are never easy to read. As I said before, the devil is always in the details.

Feathers and the Tops of Stockings—a light, cheeky image, very Helmut Newton—a bare-bottomed woman wearing stockings, a feather boa, and very little else glances knowingly back at us over her shoulder. She brings us to *the dark portal through which,* the photographer says, *so much of my work leads.*

Do I dare to eat a peach?
Are you sitting comfortably?
Then let us begin.

You can just about make out the sharp line of a table top, bisecting the picture. The predominant color is black. Beneath her stocking tops her legs disappear into blackness; above her waist is the blackness of her corset; her upper back and shoulders are a distant gray blurring into the blackness beyond. Her bottom is outlined stark and white as she bends forward over the table, haunches like two great hams. There is nothing from which one could begin to glean her state of mind.

Nothing but **My Offered Rear.**

She has no stockings on now, only a pale T-shirt and high-heeled shoes. One bare leg stands on the ground. The other is hoisted high, her right foot up on the trestle she is preparing to straddle and is gripping with both hands. A great arc cleaves the space of the picture, the left leg straight up the middle of the page, the right thigh a diagonal slash of white up into the top right-hand corner. Our eyes are inexorably drawn to the dimensional curves of her bottom and what lies in between. Only later, peering into the shadows, are we likely to register that out of a battered tin bucket, which sits on the floor beside the trestle, a hand has just drawn a **Traditional Wet Birch.**

This time, there can be no doubt, the lady really *is* getting the cane. It is there in the photograph, whipping across her bottom; a bottom that (though invisible to us) is both bared and framed by the distance between the tops of her stockings and the suspender belt that still holds them up as she bends over the bed. It is there, more particularly, in the expression on her face, caught in the very moment it lands. Her mouth is wide open, no doubt emitting some sound. So are her eyes: wide open with shock, almost certainly (I speak from experience) at the impact the cane has just made on her bottom, but also wide open with a sudden recognition.

Ah, *yes!* She *knows.*

Her look recalls that instant in Franz Kafka's The Penal Colony when the description of their crime that the machine has been so patiently inscribing on their bodies becomes legible to the condemned. The moment of enlightenment.

A picture that speaks volumes, **The Constant Examination of Self.**

And finally to a girl in high heels, black fishnet stockings with a seam running vertically up the back, pointing us straight up to her bare bottom. The stockings end about halfway up her thighs, above which line, we may assume, she will shortly make leaps and bounds in painful self-discovery. She is bending over an occasional table that supports her nicely, with her arms falling neatly down the back. Her cunt peeps demurely through. The high heels are not merely a fetish: they increase the tension in the legs, thrusting out her buttocks all the more firmly and invitingly.

Nothing restrains her. She is free to stand up, put on her clothes again, and leave whenever she wishes. But she does not.

The caption reads: **Who Am I to Understand?**

Just so.

Seconds away. King's Cross, London, 2001.

Why do these photographs suck me in? It is the swish of a rattan cane across my own behind—a cane wielded by a feminine hand—that I dream of, not the other way around. Yet photographs of men's backsides being caned would not, for me, have any of the attraction of these pictures. Is it just a matter of aesthetics: that *perfect curvature,* that *sheer dimensional beauty* of which Hamilton so lovingly writes? The female bottom as a signifier, in this matter, for my sex as well as her own? The dust dances in the sunbeams pouring through the windows of the library of McKean House, where I wait for an eternity in anticipation of being asked to *Bend over*—the cigarette smoke mingles with the steam from the showers and the dappled sunlight of an autumn afternoon, when we were very young. *She sounds just like a boy.*

Who can fathom the ways of a metaphor?

Signifiers float. That is why we can play with them—and they with us.

With slightly trembling hands, I buy the book. Woman, it is called. Later I discover that the last photograph in the collection is of a naked woman lying on her back in exactly the same posture as in Gustave Courbet's Origine du monde. Her labia look for all the world like a trunk leading to the branches and foliage that are her pubic hair.

Tree of Life.

Just a woman's genitalia. Real, symbolic, imaginary: imaginary, symbolic, real.

This one I will not leave on a railway station. *Il faut confronter des idées vagues,* says Jean-Luc Godard, *avec des images claires.*

MUM GAVE AWAY MY ROCK COLLECTION long after I had left home and such childish obsessions, I thought, behind me. I cannot blame her, though I was unaccountably miffed when I found out, years afterwards in Durham. She had passed it on to some deserving young boy who probably reminded her of me as I was then. Or maybe it was just cluttering the house, gathering dust.

Thief, thief! Baggins! We hates it for ever!

The collection was housed, as I said, in an old four-drawer document cabinet my father had filched from work. He covered the pressed cardboard with Contac, which came in rolls like wallpaper and could miraculously transform plywood into mahogany. All that was needed was faith. He had partitioned each drawer into fifteen sections, giving me space for sixty specimens in all. There was just enough room to scotchtape the name and provenance of each sample on the wooden slats that separated the compartments.

You must make sure to record exactly where each specimen was found, the Curator had impressed upon me. I was never quite sure why I should follow this scholarly obeisance, but I dutifully went through the motions.

(*Bibliography?*—the sole comment on my first undergraduate essay at Essex, scrawled in angry red.)

I was secretly disappointed when Grandad sent me the minerals from New Zealand, tiny slivers glued to a card, with no clue as to whence they came. Souvenirs bought in a shop, sullied by money.

The top drawer held the rocks, subdivided into igneous, sedimentary, and metamorphic, together with a handful of fossils. The limestones and sandstones were included for the sake of representativeness, but my heart belonged to the mottled pink granites, the black basalts. The remaining three drawers were devoted to minerals. I don't remember how they were classified, though I am certain they were. I recall only how they looked and felt. Sharp crystals of quartz, milky calcites. The lavender of amethysts. An agate like an amoeba. A flint broken open to reveal an Ali Baba's cave. Haematites shaped like kidneys that leave your hands pinky-brown, the glitter of fools' gold. Glassy micas, black and white. The long fibers of raw asbestos, the palest washed-out green.

Pristine black needles of tourmaline.

It began in Eastgate House on Rochester High Street when I was nine or ten. In the garden stood Dickens's summer house, a miniature Swiss chalet where he liked to write. I later remembered it as a supremely incongruous setting in which to dream up the spontaneous combustion of the Lord Chancellor, but it held no magic for me then. The display cases musty with medals, weapons, crockery, and hand-me-down dresses from Miss Haversham didn't much interest me either.

Just one glass cabinet in the center of the room drew me, bringing me back to gaze in wonder again and again at its contents—the unearthed treasures from King Solomon's mines, glinting like jewels from Smaug's hoard beneath the Lonely Mountain, piercing the Victorian gloom.

One day I took it into my head to knock at the Curator's door. He received me kindly, almost as if I were expected. I left with nine precious stones wrapped in tissue paper, which I carefully stowed in the saddlebag of my bike before riding off down the A2 to Sittingbourne where I laid them out on the kitchen table for Nanny and Grandad to admire.

Over the next two or three years the old man would save off-cuts for me every time something new came his way, and my collection grew. His study was dry and dusty, as was he—a man of science. But I opened him up, and he would dilate for hours over the mysteries of crystals, eyes alight.

My precioussssss.

The disappointment when that immaculate pebble you found on the beach, fresh from the sea, alive with colors, dries to an indifferent ochre.

ON THE TRAIN UP TO MILAN—before I was bushwhacked in the bookstore behind La Scala by an old acquaintance looking shapelier than ever—I read W. G. Sebald's Vertigo. Like all of Sebald's writing—I hesitate to call it fiction—the narrative meanders all over (Flaubert's syphilis, Kafka's hypochondria, Casanova's imprisonment in Venice, the author's own return to the village of his childhood in the Bavarian Alps), while being very firmly rooted in one place: in this case, Northern Italy. In The Rings of Saturn it was Norfolk, where Pa's people the Churchmans came from. The graveyard at Castleacre is full of them, Mum tells me, back to the 1700s. I read the book through my own memories. The flatlands of East Anglia—the beach at Aldeburgh, where I scavenged all day for amber—the port of Felixstowe, where a lorry driver who picked me up hitchhiking from Gillingham to Colchester one summer's day took me right on through to Rotterdam and the Hague. I smelled that sweet Dutch tobacco for the second time and sent a *Hi Mum! Look where I am now!* postcard home.

In Sebald's books there is no trajectory, no dénouement, only a perpetual circling around obscure but pregnant details and obsessively recurrent themes.

A building near the Piazza del Duomo insistently reminds me of another, dating from Maria Theresa's time, near Náměstí republiky in Prague, which in turn brings to mind Bohumil Hrabal's remark in one of his novels that you know you are at the frontier of western civilization when you step off the train at the last railway station in Galicia. I should remember when Lombardy was liberated from the Austrian yoke, but I am afraid I do not. It was too long ago. My A Levels, I mean. The threads have not all been snapped though, despite the monumental shopping arcades surmounted by the triumphal arch to Vittorio Emanuele II, Re d'Italia, a name and title that by auspicious circumstance condenses to VERDI, composer of the Risorgimento.

It is as if there were some obstinate mycelium from which strange fruits keep cropping up like fairy rings in a suburban lawn, whatever we do to try to eradicate them. My veal cutlet alla Milanese turns out to be a mere Wienerschnitzel in disguise—smažené vepřové maso, reminding me irresistibly of Prague.

In New Zealand they drive on the left-hand side of the road. My right hand kept reaching down for the gear lever that wasn't there, like an amputee scratching an itch in a phantom limb.

I have been here before. It was December 1968, and I was traveling once again with Kate, hitch-hiking back from Rome. We spent the night in the cavernous hall of Mussolini's railway station, surrounded by Fellini dwarfs.

THE YEAR, I THINK, WAS 1971. Early evening. I was out in the garden at Medway Road, making a bonfire of anything and everything that might incriminate me. Books, pamphlets, papers, letters, even some of my teenage poems. I wished now that I had not been photographed on the front page of The Daily Telegraph linking arms in the first row of a demonstration that turned into a riot. I wished I had not been at the L.S.E. the night the gates came down. Not that I had actually *done* anything. Except, perhaps, to mix up the real, the symbolic, and the imaginary even more dangerously than usual.

Two Essex University students, Anna Mendelson and Hilary Creek, had been remanded in custody for the impending Old Bailey trial of England's Fawlty Towers version of the Baader-Meinhof Gang, the Angry Brigade. None of us believed they had anything to do with the series of bombings, among them the Home Secretary's house, of which they stood indicted.

Anna features in Jean-Luc Godard's film British Sounds, part of which was shot at Essex in the spring of 1969 during a so-called Festival of Revolution of which I was one of the organizers. A young lecturer named Tim Clark, who became better known subsequently as the internationally renowned art historian and Harvard professor T. J. Clark, was rumored to be the author of a leaflet going round campus that week saying *If you see a camera smash it, it might be Godard!* I'm glad nobody took up the suggestion. The film is a fitting memorial to that hopeful and lunatic time, a time fueled by acid and fired by politics, when the best minds of my generation grasped for the heavenly connection to the starry dynamo only to find themselves sucked into the machinery of night.

If you remember the sixties, the cliché runs, *you weren't there.*

Well I do, and I was. And one thing I shall never forget was the bowel-loosening terror of that moment when the great game suddenly became sickeningly real. It was reminiscent of the night, three or four years previously, when Mick McElroy's car left the country road we were speeding from one drunken party to another: to be precise, the moment just before impact when I stopped laughing, my mouth frozen open in a silent scream. My head sheered straight down through the door handle as we ploughed into the bank, missing the tree by inches.

There but for the grace of God went Jon Cooper and Mickey Chance.

Silence; an instantaneous silence. Darkness all around us. I thought my glasses were broken, but it was only the blood, my blood, streaming down the lenses from the gash on my head. I still have the scar, just on the hairline, right in the middle of my forehead.

> *When she was good she was very, very good.*
> *But when she was bad she was horrid.*

I knew Anna Mendelson to say *Hi* to. I very much doubt she would remember me. Hilary I didn't know at all. They were both a year ahead of me, and the distance got greater when I took the 1969–70 academic year out, spending much of it abroad in Paris and India. What sent me scurrying hotfoot from Colchester back to Gillingham for an early Guy Fawkes Night was not their incarceration, but the news that two more arrests had been made. One of them was a graduate student called Chris Bott who had been my roommate for several months in my first year at Essex in a grungy loft on North Hill we shared with a Situationist Frenchman named Dominique who wore odd-colored socks, a compact girl whose name I think was Sarah, and a black Labrador called Joe whom we trained to climb ladders. A friend, of sorts, Chris. Much too close for comfort.

But the other person they arrested that day was closer to me still. It was Kate.

I could be persuaded, at a pinch, that Chris might have had some terrorist connections. He was a member of an organization called Tri-Continental, which had taken him at least once to Cuba. But Kate? It *had* to be a frame-up. And if it was a frame-up, a conspiracy fabricated out of friendships and associations, delusions and dreams of revolution, then when would they come knocking on the door for me, the third man, the missing link?

The fear is with me now, even as I write this half a lifetime later, generic, floating free, attaching itself now to this, now to that, now to

The persistence of memory. Barcelona, Spain, 2002.

the other. It never went away—even if there are times I feel safer in the bland indifference that is Canada, out of the way, the clutches of the past. *Keep a clean nose. Watch the plain clothes. You don't need a weather man to know which way the wind blows.*

Kate brought herself to the attention of Her Majesty's intelligence services, I now think, when she took off in the summer of 1969 for a revolutionary jaunt to Lebanon, spending six weeks in a Fatah training camp with an international assortment of equally idealistic young people. The girls were universally smitten by a young freedom fighter named Yasser Arafat. What is so difficult to convey, at this distance, when we have all, Arafat included, become somebody else, is the naiveté: a naiveté I must have shared since I did not at the time connect Kate's becoming a suspect in the Angry Brigade trial with her sojourn in Lebanon either.

Or was it Jordan? Now I recall it, I am sure it was Jordan.

They might just as well have been going for a vacation on an Israeli kibbutz. John Le Carré captures it perfectly. Little Drummer Girl.

The thing I admire about Kate, Tony said to me once, *is that she's very loyal. Always loyal.* Oh, **shit**. He was referring to her consideration for her two closest friends in the sixth form, a Nigerian girl called Vicky and an Indian girl called Amber, whom Kate had taken under her wing. She wasn't in the slightest political, just upper-middle-class English well-meaning, and terribly, terribly nice, caught out in a bad time. I don't mean to sound patronizing. She *was* nice, a thoroughly decent, upright English girl. It was the time that was out of joint. Tony had no idea where she was headed, and nor did I. He thought my friends in the Medway Towns too *sophisticated* for her. I, of course, was enormously flattered. He probably blamed me later for screwing up her life, and not without reason. I always did have that ability to sweep others along with me, others who sometimes lacked my intuitive knowledge of when to desert a sinking ship.

A little boy rides his bicycle into the road without looking. A young man from the village is left lying unconscious on the tarmac, far far away now and long long ago.

In the event, both Kate and Chris were acquitted on all counts—but not before they had spent the best part of a year in prison, waiting for their trial. Anna and Hilary were convicted, along with a couple of older guys I never knew. They got ten years each.

To this day I am still uncertain as to whether any such organization as the Angry Brigade ever existed outside the fevered imagination of the British security services. But the half-baked revolutionary communes peopled by directionless middle-class kids, adrift in a world that had somehow lost its moorings, they were real enough. Doris Lessing, an author of whom I am not fond, paints them without mercy or compassion in The Good Terrorist. As I keep insisting, something happened, some seismic shift in the cosmos, around the time my voice broke, and

I am not talking about miniskirts or the Beatles though they were a part of it too. Some millenarian madness was on the loose. By the later 1960s, when I went to university, it had become a raging conflagration.

The Age of Aquarius dawns.

That fire seared everybody who got too close to it. Some ended up in Brixton or Holloway, others fried their minds witless with LSD. But nobody was left without scars. The survivors were the ones who drew back from the edge. Quite a number of us traded in changing the world for *interpreting it, in various ways,* parlaying revolutionary socialism into successful academic careers. Then we tried very, very hard to forget— especially about Anna and Hilary, who were still doing their time when we got our PhDs.

I watch the young waitress set the table: two tablecloths, one laid diagonally across the other, glasses, knives, forks, spoons. The swift grace of her movements. The extraordinary beauty in the ordinary, when we make the time to stop and look at it. I am drawn once again to Wittgenstein: *philosophy leaves the world as it is.* I never thought I would live to say it, but my sympathies tonight are with Dr. Pangloss. *Il faut cultiver le jardin.* I am glad, for once, that I am no longer young—that I broke on through to the other side, as a popular song of the time urged us all to do.

Your time, she jokes. Yes, my time. Jimi, Janis, Jim, a brace of dead Kennedys. *I have a dream,* bang bang you're dead. A time raged in the shadow of Kent State and My Lai, when Apocalypse was now. A young man's time, a poet's time, a time half in love with easeful death.

NABUCCO, OR TO GIVE IT ITS FULL TITLE NABUCCODONZOR, Verdi's first big hit, premieres at La Scala on March 9, 1842. Act III. The great patriotic chorus Va, pensiero is heard for the first time. The audience erupts, demanding encore after encore. After the performance ends there is a riot. Henceforth, the Austrian authorities decree, no encores will be allowed in opera houses.

Before his death Giuseppe Verdi leaves strict instructions that no music is to be played at his funeral. Old newspaper photographs show the Piazza del Duomo packed to the walls with people, a quarter million, a half million, a million people, who will ever know? As the cortège slowly feels its way through the immense crowd somebody starts to sing, and then another, and another, and another, the words written sixty years before in another place for another time, words that they nevertheless all know by heart:

Va, pensiero, sull'ali dorate,
va, ti posa sui clivi, sui colli
ove olezzano tepide e molli
l'aure dolci del suolo natal!

A century turns.

An old coal and steel town in Northern Moravia in what was then Czechoslovakia, up near the Polish border, at the very extremity of the old Habsburg Empire. It is early in 1990, that uncertain time between the Velvet Revolution and the first free elections in forty-two years. At a loose end one evening I decide to take myself to the local opera house, where Nabucco happens to be playing. Before the performance begins a man steps through the curtain to the front of the stage. I expect to learn that one of the principals is indisposed. Instead he makes a passionate plea on behalf of his fellow-artists for the audience to vote for Civic Forum, the opposition coalition formed in November 1989 around Václav Havel.

If the communists steal the elections they'll make Cambodia look like a dinner party, somebody remarks during the interval. The tension is palpable, catching in the throat, acrid as the acid rain that hangs in the Ostrava air.

Va, pensiero is heard in absolute silence—something I have never experienced at an operatic performance anywhere in the world. No coughing, no shuffling, no whispering. Nor, I think, have I ever before or since heard a demand for a *chorus* to be encored. When the last echo of the last note dies, but not before, the theater explodes. People are on their feet, yelling for it to be played again. Va, pensiero was encored three times that night before the opera could go on. I was later told that the same thing had happened at the National Theater in Prague after the Soviet invasion of 1968, leading to Nabucco being banned from Czech stages for the next twenty years.

It was by pure coincidence that I happened to be in Milan one hundred years to the day after Giuseppe Verdi died there on January 27, 1901. I could not resist visiting the music store at La Scala, nor buying myself a CD of Claudia Muzio, whose voice I had not heard, except in my head, in years. Just for old times' sake. I was worried she would not, but she sounded *exactly* as I remembered her.

Ammogliato ... Dir che ci sono al mondo ... A pianissimo like no other. And yes it was Leoncavallo.

March 14, 1921, it was, when she stepped into an Edison studio and sang Ammogliato into the horn, the needle bobbing up and down on the revolving wax platter. Five years after the Battle of the Somme, where my great-grandfather carved the word *Bapaume* on a paper knife for his little girl Ivy.

There were intertwined ivy leaves, I seem to remember, stippled on the handle.

OH, OH, OH What a Lovely War! The most realistic film I have ever seen— with the possible exception of Lindsay Anderson's If. Haig and Joffre send wave after wave of boys up the line to death from the ballroom on Brighton Pier, posting the swelling casualties on those little moveable cards, white on black, that spell out the Hymns of the Day. The sound of an immense male choir, voices without number, wafts across the English Channel, singing the words we all know so well, Mademoiselle from Armentiers, Roses Are Blooming in Picardy, It's a Long, Long Way to Tipperary. Half a century later we are still singing them in the back row of the coach on the way home from the rugby match at Canterbury or Sevenoaks or Tunbridge Wells, *three German officers crossed the Rhine, shagged the girls and drank the wine, inky pinky parlez-vous.*

It was the autumn of 1914 I remembered, an improbably long and beautiful autumn, when the girls took to sending the boys white ribbons to shame them into enlisting. It was sobering to watch the memories click so effortlessly into overdrive. At the outset not one in ten could tell you where the Falkland Islands lay, but within a week they were engraved right there on the heart beside Dunkirk, which we all knew so well from Mrs. Miniver. *Once more into the breach dear friends.* They wait for Francis Drake to finish his game of bowls on Plymouth Hoe. Nelson puts his blind eye to his telescope. The band plays Don't Cry for Me Argentina as the Task Force sets sail from Pompey, a nice touch that, all the women are crying, mothers, wives, girlfriends, daughters. Ozzie Ardiles is booed at White Hart Lane. My left-wing Methodist lay preacher professor turns flag-waver overnight, along with many others of whom I would least have expected it. The signifiers coalesce—always the most dangerous moment. Shrieking, wheeling, hungry gulls, they alight on a barren hunk of rock in the South Atlantic and stay till they have stripped it bare, drowning out all rhyme and reason with their din.

A ship full of teenage Argentine conscripts is dispatched to Davy Jones's locker.

Gotcha! screams The Sun.

Appalled, I write a letter to The Times, protesting *the sinking of the General Belgrano, with the probable loss of several hundred lives.* The last refuge of the middle-class Englishman, pissing in the wind. I feel like King Canute sitting in his deckchair on Brighton beach beneath the Prince Regent's oriental pavilion, commanding the sea to recede. Every death creates a need for another, an eye for an eye and a tooth for a tooth, otherwise *What did they die for?* Until we have had our fill of deaths, that is: but this is early days yet, Run Rabbit Run and We'll Hang Out Our Washing on the Siegfried Line days.

It is not as if I haven't been here before.

> *What passing bells for these who die as cattle?*
> *Only the monstrous anger of the guns.*
> *Only the stuttering rifles' rapid rattle*
> *Can patter out their hasty orisons.*

Years later, Philip Corrigan's eyes mist over in a pub in Oxford, quite possibly the Eagle and Child, but then again most probably not. He tells me of the dignity of Margaret Thatcher's farewell speech to Parliament after they dumped her as leader, the Tory rabble of second-rate jobbers and second-hand dealers snapping at her heels. He was as sad and angry as I have ever seen him, my dear Philip—Philip, a lifelong opponent of all Margaret Thatcher stood for, *Philip,* who will to his dying day believe in the possibility of human capacities perfecting social forms in a way I know I never again shall. But I felt exactly the same. A piece of ourselves was becoming history.

Gotcha! Gotcha by the short and curlies, gotcha right there in the heart. Wasn't that exactly what we were trying to get our heads around in The Great Arch?

The persistence of memory, carried across chasms of time and space on the golden wings of the most unlikely of signifiers, in wax, in sepia, in stone. Salvador Dalí painted it accurately in all its surreality. We are nothing without it. Yet it frightens me in these old places where people remember their histories in the same way that my fingers remember how to move across the keyboard of a computer—that my right hand reaches down to shift gear—that my bottom, no more voluntarily, craves the childhood sting of a rattan cane. I fear it because of its immense power to move us, snatching us up and spiriting us God knows where before we even know it. Like China Hamilton's oh-so-lucid pictures, over which I lingered so long in the bookstore in Milan. Like that lump in my throat in Auckland, brought on by the word *Gallipoli* and a list of place-names of which I had never, until that moment, heard.

Is it any wonder if sometimes I feel I am being remembered, recollected, recalled—that the hand that jerks me is not mine?

A line is uttered on the stage and she begins to scream uncontrollably, without knowing why.

ONE OF THE LAST TIMES I spoke with Daniel on the phone, pissed that he made me miss half of NYPD Blue, I cut the conversation short. He never got off the plane, that night in Edmonton. I had my truck radio tuned to CISN FM, the country music station. I thought it would amuse him to see me in my native habitat. We had only ever met up in faraway places: Pasadena, New York, San Diego, Chicago, Oxford. Later that night I get a phone call. His voice comes through, long distance: deep, hesitant, gravelly from the incessant Camels he smoked unfiltered, another holdout against the Puritan tide. That slow Utah drawl. I remember voices far better than I do faces, and Dan's voice was unmistakable. But it was not Daniel on the other end of the line, it was his brother Stephen, and he was calling me from London, England, not Tucson, Arizona.

I have never heard two voices sound so uncannily alike. We canceled the talk Dan was to have given at the university without explanation.

So the dude didn't show? a colleague asked me a few days later.

No, I said, *the dude didn't show.*

I've been here before, too.

A thirteen-year-old boy is walking along the road by the cathedral cloisters up to Minor Canon Row, trailing his fingers along the black painted railings. I can't now remember where he was going or why. The boy has recently lost his grandmother, to whom he was as close as any human being on earth. The last time he saw her, apart from that time when she squeezed his hand in the hospital, was the day John F. Kennedy was shot and all the women were crying; so that day, although he doesn't know it yet, will be seared on his memory, just as it will, for equally

Self-portrait in dubious company. Siena, 2001.

personal reasons, on the memories of the rest of his generation. He is not very good at coping with death. Yesterday he made some clever taunt at somebody else's expense about *teaching my grandmother to suck eggs,* adding, just for effect, *and she's dead!* It raised a laugh. He immediately felt ashamed of himself. He didn't let it show though. He knows how to tough it out. Boys don't cry. *Ever.*

The sun is shining and the rain is falling, all at once, great warm raindrops falling on his head. The boy slows down, raises his face to the sky, and lets the rain pour in torrents down his cheeks.

Where I was happiest in Milan was in the Emporio Armani, a space light, bright, airy, and utterly, utterly frivolous.

IT WAS LATE AFTERNOON as she and I took the coast road from Brighton to Eastbourne. I was disappointed, inevitably. A line kept coming to mind about England being *all bricked up now.* But there were reassurances. Roedean, the Victorian girls' public school whose existence I had forgotten, still stared lonely and forbidding from the high cliffs out to sea. Rottingdean, the dip in the road, the fold in the hills, the art deco cinema, was just as I remembered it. We drove quickly on through Newhaven. The curve of the road into Seaford was unexpectedly, intimately familiar—the more affecting because I had completely forgotten the moment of excitement that came with knowing that we were *nearly there*. I caught my breath at the sight of Seaford Head hunched over at the far end of the beach, beyond the Martello tower. Nothing had changed, it seemed. I continued to feel this even as I drove the length of the front, searching eagerly for the Esplanade Hotel and finding only tacky North American condominiums.

The English long ago forsook the Sussex coast for Benidorm, Tenerife, and all points west. I didn't really think I would find the hotel, still less the vacant lot behind the Esplanade annex where Alison and I flicked cigarette cards against a wall more than forty years ago. She pitched all the carefully collected cards into the sea the day we left. That must have been in our fifth or sixth summer there, the summer of Cliff Richard and Del Shannon.

No, what disconcerted me was not the vanished hotel, but the absence of breakwaters—*the bleached breakwaters marching into the sea, green and barnacled and slimy below the waterline*—which were as enduring a fixture of my memories of the English seaside as cockles and candyfloss. There were no breakwaters to be seen, just the long sloping shingle.

> *Listen! You hear the grating roar*
> *Of pebbles which the waves draw back, and fling,*
> *At their return, up the high strand,*
> *Begin, and cease, and then again begin,*
> *With tremulous cadence slow, and bring*
> *The eternal note of sadness in.*

Back home in Canada, I rummaged through old photographs my mother gave me in New Zealand. I found a creased black-and-white print, probably taken on a Kodak Brownie, of me, Alison, and Neil in bathing costumes sitting on a breakwater as if we were riding a rocking horse. Our ages, I would guess, are seven, four, and eighteen months. Neil is looking out to sea, Alison and I into the camera. On the back of the photograph, in my mother's hand, is written the single word *Seaford*.

On top of the world. Brynderwyn Heads, New Zealand, 2000.

Conclusive evidence for the reliability of my memory? Hardly. For Mum has also written *Seaford* on many other photographs, some of which were clearly taken elsewhere.

A picture of Mum, Alison, and me scrabbling on a pebble beach dates from a couple of years earlier. Alison has a toque around her head, and the hood of my duffle coat is up. Mum is wrapped in a heavy knee-length coat and her hair is blowing in the wind. She looks very young and very pretty. The beach is deserted, the sea rough. A typical English day at the seaside, that coldness I can recall sharply enough to want to write about it four decades later. But the picture was not taken at Seaford at all, but a few miles up the coast at Birling Gap—the white cliffs in the background are unmistakably the Seven Sisters.

We detoured to Birling Gap last summer too. My fiftieth. I remembered the view along the shoreline, which is unchanged, but had absolutely no recollection of the terraced houses at the top of the cliff, which must have been there since the nineteenth century.

I am wearing the same duffle coat in another photograph, busy making a sandcastle with a plastic bucket and spade. On the back Mum has written *Seaford. 4 years.* But Seaford's beach was entirely shingle—and behind me is a pier, which Seaford certainly never possessed. Brighton, or maybe Eastbourne, I would guess, but who knows?

A final picture, of my grandmother holding my brother as a baby, shows what *could* just be the front at Seaford—the sharp slope of the beach is right, the silhouette of the houses rings a distant bell—and further down the beach *is* a breakwater. Mum's caption reads *Nanny and Neil.*

It might be anywhere.

It would be easy enough, I imagine, to check up on whether or not there actually were breakwaters in the late 1950s which have since been removed or just rotted away, or whether I have unwittingly imported the particulars of Herne Bay or Selsey or Canvey Island into Seaford, the better to remember it.

But to do so would be to miss the point.

NOTES

René Magritte, "The Treachery of Images." Magritte painted more than one picture with this title. The one I was looking at, painted in 1952–53, is reproduced in Robert Hughes (ed.), *The Portable Magritte*, New York: Universe, p. 314.

"You're never alone with a Strand." Advertising slogan for cigarettes, Britain, 1959. The black-and-white TV ad featured the actor Terence Brooks, wearing a trench coat and a hat on the back of his head and looking like Frank Sinatra on the cover of the classic *In the Wee Small Hours* album (1955), stopping to light a cigarette. The music, by Cliff Adams, was later released (by popular demand) under the title "Lonely Man Theme."

Albert Camus, *The Fall*, New York: Vintage, 1991.

"Female smells ..." T. S. Eliot, "Rhapsody on a Windy Night," in his *Collected Poems 1909–1962*, London: Faber and Faber, 1974, p. 28.

George Orwell, *Keep the Aspidistra Flying*, 1936. All the Orwell books referred to in this text are available in *The Penguin Complete Novels of George Orwell*, London: Penguin, 1983.

Len Deighton, *The Ipcress File*, London: Hodder and Stoughton, 1962. The hero is never named in the book. In Sidney J. Furie's 1965 film, where the spy was played by Michael Caine, he becomes his alias Harry Palmer.

Chet Baker, the jazz trumpeter and singer, died falling out of a window of a hotel in Amsterdam on May 13, 1988. Whether he jumped, slipped, or was pushed has never been determined, but he was likely high on drugs.

Dennis Potter, *Blue Remembered Hills*, a TV play that first aired on BBC in January 1979. Two other TV works by Potter, *Pennies from Heaven*

(1978) and *Lipstick on my Collar* (1993), have also lodged deep in my memory, with their unique mixture of the surreal and the nostalgic, and—above all perhaps—their inventive use of popular songs. Potter's last interview, with Melvyn Bragg on the Channel 4 program *Without Walls* in 1994, was well nigh unbearable to watch; the dying playwright alternated glasses of white wine and doses of morphine for the pancreatic cancer he called "Rupert" (after Rupert Murdoch). He had declined other treatment.

Elizabeth David. I learned to cook from her books, and possess most of them, but cannot track down this remark, though I am sure she said it. She writes beautifully—comparably with M. F. K. Fisher among American cookery writers. For a sample see *An Omelette and A Glass of Wine* (London: Penguin, 1986) or *Is There a Nutmeg in the House?* (London: Michael Joseph, 2000).

"Keep The Home Fires Burning" (1914, lyricist Lena Guilbert Ford) and "We'll Gather Lilacs in the Spring Again" (from *Perchance to Dream*, 1945) were both composed by Ivor Novello. An Internet search throws up *no* recordings of "We'll Gather Lilacs" by Vera Lynn, whose great wartime classic was—of course—"We'll Meet Again."

"Though you might hear laughin' ... Take me disappearin' ..." Bob Dylan, "Mr. Tambourine Man," on the album *Bringing It All Back Home* (1965).

"There are, indeed, things ..." Ludwig Wittgenstein, *Tractatus Logico-Philosophicus*, London: Routledge and Kegan Paul, 1971, p. 151.

"What set him off ..." See Marcel Proust, *The Way by Swann's*, volume 1 of *In Search of Lost Time*, London: Allen Lane, 2003, pp. 46–50.

Carry On Up the Khyber, 1968. British comedy film, one of a lengthy series of "*Carry On*" movies, starring Sidney James as Sir Sidney Ruff-Diamond and Kenneth Williams as the Khasi of Kalabar (a *khazi* being British slang for a toilet).

"What should they know of England ..." Rudyard Kipling, "The English Flag," in *Rudyard Kipling's Verse: Definitive Edition*, New York: Doubleday, 1940, p. 221.

"While My Guitar Gently Weeps." A song on The Beatles' so-called White Album (which was actually titled simply "The Beatles"), 1968.

"Like a Rolling Stone." A song on Bob Dylan's album *Highway 61 Revisited* (1965), which I listened to often in India.

"Footfalls echo in the memory." T. S. Eliot, "Burnt Norton," the first of *The Four Quartets*, London: Faber and Faber, 1983, pp. 13–14.

René Magritte, "La Condition Humaine." Again, Magritte painted more than one picture with this title. The one I had in mind, painted in 1933, is reproduced in *The Portable Magritte*, p. 139.

David Dale, Robert Owen. Details from *Dictionary of National Biography*.

School report: direct quotations. The letter from the headmaster to my parents is quoted from memory. "A" (Advanced) Levels were the final exams in high school, necessary for university entrance, normally sat at age eighteen. The minimum school leaving age in Britain then was still fifteen.

"A thing of beauty ..." John Keats, from "Endymion," in *The Albatross Book of Verse*, edited by Louis Untermeyer, London: Collins, 1960, page 369.

"Heard melodies ..." John Keats, "Ode on a Grecian Urn," in *The Albatross Book of Verse*, page 375.

La Passionara. Dolores Ibarruri, a communist heroine of the Spanish Civil War.

Working-class heroes. Glasgow got the name "Red Clydeside" because of the militancy of its labor movement during and after World War I. But I suspect there is also an echo here of both John Lennon's 1970 song "Working-Class Hero" and the Scottish director Bill Forsythe's 1983 film *Local Hero*.

"The inexhaustible productive powers of modern industry." Karl Marx and Friedrich Engels, *Manifesto of the Communist Party*, in their *Collected Works*, Vol. 6, London: Lawrence and Wishart, 1976. I cannot find this exact phrase anywhere in the text, though the sentiment is there in abundance. Given that I spent many years of my life reading and writing about Karl Marx (*Marx's Method*, 1979; *The Violence of Abstraction*, 1986; *Readings from Karl Marx*, 1988; *Capitalism and Modernity*, 1991), I find the misattribution intriguing.

"We have long forgotten ..." Walter Benjamin, "One-Way Street," in his *Selected Writings*, Vol. 1, Cambridge: Belknap Press, 1996, p. 445.

Bob Hope, the American comedian, was still alive when I wrote this. He finally died at the age of one hundred on July 27, 2003.

Oscar Wilde, *The Picture of Dorian Grey*, Ware: Wordsworth Editions, 2001. "The nineteenth-century dislike of realism," writes Wilde in the Preface, "is the rage of Caliban seeing his own face in a glass. The nineteenth-century dislike of romanticism is the rage of Caliban not seeing his own face in a glass" (p. 3).

Wipers. British World War I soldiers' slang for the town of Ypres.

Rightaway. Right of way, of course—but this was how my pre-literate self heard and remembered it. It was a lane at the end of the gardens.

"Punishment will come ..." Anne Rice, *The Claiming of Sleeping Beauty*, New York: Plume, 1999, pp. 25–26.

"Remember the baths ... I awoke." George Seferis, from "Mythical Story," in *Four Greek Poets*, edited and translated by Edmund Keeley and Philip Sherrard, Harmondsworth: Penguin, 1966, p. 44.

"Visions of Johanna" and "Desolation Row." Songs on Bob Dylan's albums *Blonde on Blonde* (1966) and *Highway 61 Revisited* respectively.

"Having known this fate ..." Seferis, "Mythical Story," p. 53.

Pausanias, *Guide to Greece*, c. 150–170 A.D., translated by Peter Levi, Harmondsworth: Penguin, 1979.

"Zadok the Priest." G. F. W. Handel, one of four anthems composed for the coronation of George II in 1727 and performed at every subsequent coronation of a British monarch.

"The people that walked ..." *The Holy Bible,* King James Authorized Version, Isaiah 9, verses 2 and 6.

"Sing we then the school of Roffa." King's School Rochester school song.

St. Peter's College, Oxford; a place I have visited regularly now, as much to keep friendships alive as for academic purposes, for some twenty-five years. My first contact with the college was through Gavin Williams, who moved there from Durham in the late 1970s, Philip Corrigan, with whom I co-authored three books (*Socialist Construction and Marxist Theory, For Mao,* and *The Great Arch*) and established *The Journal of Historical Sociology,* and the late Gerald Aylmer, who was the College Master. Together we set up the long-running annual historians' workshop known simply as the Discussion Group on the State. See the note I wrote, by way of an obituary for Gerald, "Gerald Aylmer and DGOS: In Memoriam," in *The Journal of Historical Sociology,* vol. 15, no. 1, 2002, pp. 60–66. The memorial service for Gerald, which took place in the University Church in 2001, might well have found its way into this memoir. Certainly it belongs. Gavin ushered in the large congregation at the door; Sir Keith Thomas gave a splendid address, quoting among other things George Melly's *Rum, Bum, and Concertina;* and the sun flooded through the suitably puritan plain high windows, as we sang lustily for those in peril on the sea.

Guy Fawkes Night (or Bonfire Night). Every November 5 in Britain bonfires are lit, fireworks are set off, and Guy Fawkes, a conspirator in the so-called Gunpowder Plot to blow up the Houses of Parliament in 1605, is burned in effigy. The old joke runs that he was the only man ever to enter parliament with honest intentions.

"The ancient dead ..." Seferis, "Mythical Story." This is *not* among the selections I first read from "Mythical Story" in *Four Greek Poets.* The couplet is from poem #21 in the cycle, which is available in the later full English translation under the title "Mythistorema" in George Seferis, *Collected Poems,* Princeton: Princeton University Press, 1995, p. 25—which I read much later.

Nellie Melba's "Ave Maria," recorded on July 7, 1906, can be heard on *Nellie Melba: The London Recordings 1904–1926* (The HMV Treasury, 1976). Alison Stamp sings the treble line on *Allegri: Miserere* (re-released on CD, Gimmel, 2001), with the Tallis Scholars. Contrary to what I recollected, it was recorded in Merton College Chapel, Oxford, not in King's College, Cambridge.

"My friend Daniel." The anthropologist Daniel Nugent, author of *Spent Cartridges of Revolution* (Chicago University Press, 1994), and an editor of *The Journal of Historical Sociology.* The last of the long-haired boys was Gavin Williams's fond description of him. He was active in theater and played guitar in a band, as well as being an accomplished and unusually courageous academic. Daniel died, suddenly and utterly unexpectedly, in October 1997, at the age of forty-three.

Ten-bob note. Ten-shilling note.

Fags. English slang for cigarettes.

Rudyard Kipling, *Puck of Pook's Hill*, London: Macmillan, 1951.

The Beatles, *Sergeant Pepper's Lonely Hearts Club Band*, 1967.

Lady Bracknell, "A handbag?" In Oscar Wilde, *The Importance of Being Ernest*.

Fly half: position in rugby.

BFPO. British Forces Post Office. "Two-Way Family Favourites," which ran on BBC radio from 1945 to 1980, played requests for military families. At its height it had an audience of twenty million in Britain and seven million in Germany.

"P.S. I love you," a much-requested early Beatles song. From the album *Please Please Me* (March 1963).

"We have lingered ..." T. S. Eliot, "The Love Song of J. Alfred Prufrock," in *Collected Poems*, p. 17.

Mines of Moria. J. R. R. Tolkien, *The Fellowship of the Ring*, London: HarperCollins, 1991, book 2, chapters 4 and 5 (Moria); p. 95 (mushrooms), p. 99 ("O blessed Meriadoc"). I have mixed up these latter two incidents.

Wittgenstein, *Tractatus*, p. 151.

"I only have one language ..." Jacques Derrida, *Monolingualism of the Other, or The Prosthesis of Origin*. Stanford: Stanford University Press, 1998, p. 1.

"Prince Andrey wakes up ..." In Leo Tolstoy, *War and Peace*, New York: Modern Library, 2002, pp. 312–313. It was Austerlitz, not Borodino.

Chinooks. Warm winds, skirting the Rocky Mountains, which suddenly drive up the Alberta temperatures in the middle of a frigid prairie winter.

Edward Hopper, "Gas" (1940), reproduced in Gail Levin, *Edward Hopper: The Art and the Man*, New York: Norton, 1980, p. 208.

Nodding donkeys. Contraptions that pump oil that litter Alberta farmlands, so called from the way they nod up and down.

The Edmonton tornado struck in the afternoon of July 1, 1987, leaving twenty-seven dead and over $300 million in property damage.

Wayne Gretzky. The (ice) hockey player known simply as The Great One, who took the Edmonton Oilers to four Stanley Cups between 1984 and 1988, was traded to the L.A. Kings on August 9, 1988, for the unheard-of figure of $15 million. *Sports Illustrated* described it as "the biggest trade in the history of sport." *The Edmonton Journal* ran its deepest, blackest headline since the end of World War II: "GRETZKY GONE!"

"And 'Tea!' she said ..." John Betjeman, "Death in Leamington," in *John Betjeman's Collected Poems*, London: John Murray, 1962, p. 2.

Mrs. Rochester. A character in Charlotte Bronte's *Jane Eyre,* whom Jean Rhys in turn took as the basis for her 1966 novel *Wide Sargasso Sea.*

Agatha Christie, *Sleeping Murder* (1976), one of her many Miss Marple books.

John Webster, *The Duchess of Malfi,* first performed in 1613 or 1614.

Beachy Head. A cliff near Eastbourne in Sussex, the highest in England.

Seige of Gondor, battle of the Pellenor Fields. Incidents in J. R. R. Tolkien, *The Return of the King,* London: HarperCollins, 1991, book 5, chapters 4 and 6.

"Goodbye Piccadilly ..." From "A Long Way to Tipperary," composed by Jack Judge and Harry Williams in 1912. This became one of the most popular soldiers' songs of World War I.

Fid. Def. Ind. Imp. Defender of the faith, Emperor of India. Latin abbreviations in inscriptions on English coins still circulating in my childhood.

Going down for air. The echo, of course, is of George Orwell's 1939 novel *Coming Up for Air.*

James Bond, Ian Fleming's secret agent 007. *Thunderball* was published in 1961.

Richard Adams, *Maia.* New York: Knopf, 1995.

Pablo Picasso's depictions of cunnilingus include the watercolors "Erotic Scene" of 1902 (blue) and "Two Figures and a Cat" of 1902–03 (pink), reproduced in Jean Clair (ed.), *Picasso Erotique,* Munich: Prestel, 2001, pp. 170 and 173 respectively.

Gustave Courbet, "L'origine du monde," 1866. Once owned by Jacques Lacan, the painting is now on permanent exhibit in the Musée d'Orsay.

"Seven Steps to Heaven." The recording I am recollecting was on the album *Miles Davis Greatest Hits,* which was re-released, much expanded, as a Columbia CD in 1997.

Nobuyoshi Araki, *Tokyo Lucky Hole,* Köln: Taschen, 1997. *Art at the Turn of the Millenium* and *1000 Chairs* are also published by Taschen, whose extensive list effectively mass-markets both art and erotica in several languages.

Alberto Moravia, "The Belt," in his *Erotic Tales,* New York: Farrar Straus & Giroux, 1983.

W. G. Sebald, *The Rings of Saturn,* New York: New Directions, 1999, pp. 159ff.

Robert Coover, *Spanking the Maid,* New York: Grove Press, 1998.

Robert Nye, *Merlin,* New York: Bantam, 1981.

"Any Malaysian climbing plant ..." *The Oxford English Dictionary,* entry on rattan.

"It was at the end of the eighteenth century ..." Edward Anthony, *Thy Rod and Staff,* London: Abacus, 1997, p. 229.

Abandoned the theories ... T. S. Eliot, "The Triumph of Bullshit," in his

Inventions of the March Hare: Poems 1909–1917, New York: Harcourt Brace, 1998, p. 307. His poem "The Love Song of St. Sebastian," in the same collection of work that was unpublished during his lifetime, is also interesting in the present context: "I would come with a lamp in the night / And sit at the foot of your stair / I would flog myself until I bled / And after hour on hour of prayer / And torture and delight / Until my blood should ring the lamp / And glisten in the light" (pp. 78–79).

Jean-Jacques Rousseau famously relates how on being spanked by the thirty-year-old Mlle. Lambercier at age eight he "found in the suffering, even in the shame, an admixture of sensuality which had left me with more desire than fear to experience it again from the same hand"—an experience, he believed, that "determined my tastes, my desires, my passions, myself for the rest of my life." *The Confessions and Correspondence,* edited and translated by Christopher Kelly, Hanover: University Press of New England, 1995, pp. 13–16. He continues: "It is not what is criminal that costs the most to tell, it is what is ridiculous and shameful" (p. 15).

"Do I dare to eat a peach?" Eliot, "Prufrock." *Collected Poems,* p. 17.

Tobermory and Penang. See Yoke-Sum Wong, "The Sigh of the East: A Sense of Empire and Other Lingerings," in *Canadian Review of Sociology and Anthropology,* vol. 36, no. 2, May 1999.

"How do I love thee? Let me count the ways." Elizabeth Barrett Browning, *Sonnets from the Portuguese,* Mount Vernon: Peter Pauper Press, p. 54.

Home and Colonial. The name of a chain of grocery stores in England in my childhood, which had been a feature of the English landscape since the late Victorian period.

"Remember, remember ..." See above, p. 120, Guy Fawkes Night.

The Gang Show was started by Ralph Reader at the Palace Theatre in Holborn, London, in 1932. It became an annual event, and subsequently "Gang Shows" spread throughout the international scouting movement. Notable British entertainers who performed in Gang Shows in their youth include Sir Harry Secombe, Sir Richard Attenborough, Peter Sellers, Max Bygraves, Spike Milligan, Dick Emery, and Tony Hancock.

"Strolling, just strolling ..." was one of the signature tunes (along with "Underneath the Arches") of the British music-hall duo Bud Flanagan and Chesney Allen, who as part of the Crazy Gang dominated the stage of the London Palladium in the 1930s and '40s.

"By the light of the silvery moon ..." Another music-hall favorite, written by Edward Madden and Gus Edwards in 1909.

"Run, rabbit, run." Written by Noel Gaye, this was a big hit for Flanagan and Allen in 1939. It was inspired by the first German bomb to be dropped on England during World War II, which landed harmlessly in a farmer's field.

The Two Fat Ladies. (Very) English TV cooking show, networked in

North America (where I first saw it) in 1997. Clarissa Dickson Wright and the late Jennifer Paterson were the hosts.

"By roads not adopted ... Miss J. Hunter Dunn ... Love-thirty ... strongly adorable ... on the floor of her bedroom ..." John Betjeman, "A Subaltern's Love Song," in *John Betjeman's Collected Poems*, pp. 105–107.

Sirens. 1994 film, directed by John Duigan, of which Hugh Grant was the co-star.

La vice anglaise. French term for spanking. Not entirely unjustified: prominent English figures who were fascinated by the sexual allure of corporal punishment include W. E. Gladstone, T. E. Lawrence, Algernon Swinburne, Philip Larkin, the theater critic Kenneth Tynan, and the painter Francis Bacon—not that the French lack their own aficionados, from Sade to Apollinaire (see his *Lettres à Lou* or, at tedious length, *Onze mille vierges*). English erotic literature is particularly rich in spanking scenes, from the encounter between Fanny and Mr. Barvile (a young man "unaccountably condemn'd to have his pleasure lashed into him, as boys have their learning") in John Cleland's *Fanny Hill* (first published in 1748–49; London: Penguin, 1985, quotation from p. 182) onward. The English vice is also the butt of a good deal of vulgar comedy, as in one British TV show I saw—I can't remember which show or when—in which a Conservative politician's wife greets him after a hard day in the Commons with the lines: "You've done so well, darling, I'm going to give you a jolly good spanking! *And* you can watch 'Baywatch'!" The choice of the rattan cane as the queen of disciplinary implements seems a peculiarly English fetish.

"Fine tang of faintly scented urine." James Joyce, *Ulysses*, London: The Bodley Head, 1967, p. 65.

With Clive at Plassey, etc. The reference is to the novels of G. A. Henty. The Famous Five and The Secret Seven are heroes of children's books by Enid Blyton. Harry Wharton and his friends are characters in the Greyfriars school novels of Frank Richards, starring the "Fat Owl" Billy Bunter. Captain W. E. Johns's Biggles books belong here too, along with Paul Brickhill's *Reach for the Sky*. Character-builders all.

Dyb dyb dyb. Cub scout ritual. Akela; leader of cub scout pack, from Rudyard Kipling's *The Jungle Book*.

Puck, Dan, and Una. Characters in Kipling's *Puck of Pook's Hill*.

"I am sick o' wastin' leather ..." Rudyard Kipling, "Mandalay," *Rudyard Kipling's Verse*, p. 417.

Calgary. The Canadian city is named after the beach on the Isle of Mull in Scotland, of which Tobermory is the main town.

Nawab of Pataudi, Harold Larwood. Legendary cricketers. The Ashes is the name given to the bi-annual cricket matches between England and Australia played since 1882, when England lost to an Australian Eleven at the Oval and *The Sporting Times* published the following obituary:

In Affectionate Remembrance
of
E N G L I S H C R I C K E T,
which died at the Oval
on
29th A U G U S T, 1882,
Deeply lamented by a large circle of sorrowing friends and acquaintances
R.I.P.
N.B.—The body will be cremated and the ashes taken to Australia.

The miner Harold Larwood's so-called "bodyline" bowling won England the Ashes in 1932–33. He refused to apologize for his aggressive bowling, and never played for England again. Many would conclude there were class issues involved, of the "gentleman" vs. "players" variety. The Nawab of Pataudi (b. 1941), Wisden Cricketer of the Year in 1968, was by common consent India's greatest captain ever. He also played for the English county of Sussex.

"The Hillman is waiting ..." Betjeman, "Subaltern's Love-Song," p. 106.

"When I see a couple of kids ... Rather than words comes the thought ..." Philip Larkin, "High Windows," in his *Collected Poems,* New York: Farrar, Straus, Giroux, 1993, p. 165.

René Magritte, "The False Mirror." Again, there is more than one painting with this title. The one referred to here, painted in 1929, is reproduced in *The Portable Magritte,* p. 114.

Merry and Pippin smoking at Isengard. J. R. R. Tolkien, *The Two Towers,* London: HarperCollins, 1991, pp. 543–544.

Eagle and Child. An Oxford pub, known affectionately as "the Bird and Baby," in which Lewis, Tolkien, and the rest of the Inklings (as they called themselves) met. See Humphrey Carpenter, *The Inklings: C. S. Lewis, J. R. R. Tolkien, Charles Williams, and Their Friends,* Houghton Mifflin: Ballantine, 1978. Philip and Daniel: Daniel Nugent, Philip Corrigan.

"Ah love, let us be true ..." Matthew Arnold, "Dover Beach." in *The Centuries' Poetry,* Vol. 4, *Hood to Hardy,* edited by Denys Killam Roberts, Harmondsworth: Penguin, 1950, pp. 105–107.

Derek Sayer, *Capitalism and Modernity: An Excursus on Marx and Weber,* London: Routledge, 1991, p. 134.

Tethered Moon, *Chansons d'Edith Piaf.* Winter & Winter Records, 1999.

Little piece of ivory. In her letter to her nephew James Edward Austen of December 16, 1816, Jane Austen wrote self-deprecatingly of "the little bit (two Inches wide) of Ivory on which I work with so fine a brush, as pro–duces little effect after much labour." Jane Austen, *Letters 1796–1817,* edited by R. W. Chapman, Oxford University Press, 1955, p. 189.

Lust Corner. Noel Akchoté, Eugene Chadbourne, Marc Ribot, Winter & Winter Records, 1997.

"My love she speaks like silence ..." Bob Dylan, "Love minus zero/No limit," on *Bringing It All Back Home.*

"Shine On You Crazy Diamond." A song by Pink Floyd, on their 1975 album *Wish You Were Here.*

Lucinda Williams, "Side of the Road," on her album *Lucinda Williams* (Koch Records, 1998).

"I saw the best minds ..." The opening lines of Allen Ginsberg's "Howl," in his *Howl and Other Poems,* San Francisco: City Lights Books, 1991.

Karl Marx lived with his family in Dean Street from 1851 to 1856, probably the most poverty-stricken years of his life. The housekeeper was Helene (Lenchen) Demuth, their illegitimate son Frederick Demuth, born in June 1851. Engels accepted paternity at the time, but named Marx as the true father to Marx's daughter Eleanor on his deathbed.

Marxists and Oxford Colleges: I had in mind Christopher Hill. The famous painter is Francis Bacon.

"Bring me my bow ..." William Blake, the hymn "Jerusalem" (as I first knew it), from his "Milton," in *The Centuries' Poetry,* Vol. 3, Pope to Keats, edited by Denys Kilham Roberts, Harmondsworth: Penguin, 1950, p. 119.

Colin Richmond, "The Survivors: My Last Sixty-Six Long Playing Records—For Ray Smith and Bob Glass," *The Journal of Historical Sociology,* vol. 13, no. 1, March 2000. Dobell's led me to "The Survivors," but Colin actually interweaves his father's death and Dobell's in another text, which I in turn read back into "The Survivors." I cannot resist quoting the passage here: "Here I would want to describe the uncomplicated incident at Lamorbey of a steepling six and a next-ball out, which took place between the death of my father and his funeral. He died on Thursday 24 April 1986. On Saturday 26 April I went to do a morning's work in the Manuscripts Room of the British Library, a place of refuge and refreshment, and on the way back to Charing Cross stopped at Dobell's new shop just behind Cambridge Circus. I bought there the 1985 Swedish Dragon long-playing record of the Miles Davis and John Coltrane concerts in Stockholm in 1960. I still have the sleeve: the magenta sticker says £12.95. By the time I am in Sidcup it is a balmy afternoon. I walk from the station through the glade and there on my right in the grounds of Lamorbey House a cricket match is in progress: as I pass the batsman clouts an enormous six and I stop to watch his next effort. He is clean bowled. The power of this memory, its indelibility indeed, is created by the realization that I cannot share the moment with my dear father: Blessed Be He." "Synopsis for a Book on Cricket in Twenty-Four Parts," *The Journal of Historical Sociology,* vol. 13, no. 4, 2000, p. 443. Colin is an eminent historian of late-medieval England. He is also a marvelous writer of less academic—but no less historical—pieces (of which these are examples). Several have been published in *The Journal of Historical Sociology* and *Common Knowledge.* They are very well worth searching out.

George Smiley. The hero of several of John Le Carré's espionage novels, including the great trilogy *Tinker, Tailor, Soldier, Spy* (1974), *The Honourable Schoolboy* (1977), *and Smiley's People* (1980). Earlier Smiley novels are *Call for the Dead (1961)*, and *A Murder of Quality (1962)*. The latter is a detective story set in an English boys' preparatory school, which I found extraordinarily evocative.

Swish and *Sting* are (or were) English spanking magazines.

The chance encounter between an umbrella and a sewing machine. A famous image, seized on by André Breton and the surrealists, from Isadore Ducasse, Comte de Lautréamont's *Chants de Maldoror* (1869).

"Let us go then, you and I ..." T. S. Eliot, "Prufrock," in *Collected Poems*, p. 13. The "violet skies" image is also his, but I have forgotten where it comes from.

George Orwell, *A Clergyman's Daughter*, in the *Complete Novels*, pp. 255–256. I have misremembered the opening of the novel here; something I return to later (p. 55).

"Between the end of the Chatterley ban ..." Philip Larkin, "Annus Mirabilis," in his *Collected Poems*, p. 167.

"In the bleak midwinter ..." Christina Rossetti, "A Christmas Carol," in her *Goblin Market*, London: Phoenix, 1996, p. 45.

"That syrupped all her face ... Eat me, drink me ..." Christina Rossetti, *Goblin Market*, pp. 39, 40.

"We have no rivers ..." Seferis, "Mythical Story," p. 50.

Geoffrey Grigson, *The Goddess of Love: The Birth, Triumph, Death and Return of Aphrodite*, London: Quartet, 1978. The statue, a Graeco-Roman copy from Nero's Golden House at Rome of a Hellenistic original, is pictured on p. 96.

"We find it strange ..." Seferis, "Mythical Story," p. 50.

Del Shannon's song "Runaway" was a huge hit in England in 1961.

Bertold Brecht, *The Threepenny Novel*, Harmondsworth: Penguin, 1961.

"By full tilt river ..." Dylan Thomas, "Poem on His Birthday," in his *Collected Poems 1934–1952*, New York: New Directions, p. 190.

Radio Caroline begun broadcasting on Easter Sunday 1964, the first of the "pirate" radio stations whose huge success forced the BBC to introduce the largely pop music Radio 1 in 1967. Radio 1 subsequently hired many of the pirate radio DJs, including Tony Blackburn. The actress Tessa Wyatt was his then girlfriend.

"Her body had gone goose-flesh all over ..." Orwell, *A Clergyman's Daughter*, p. 256.

"Fool of a Took!" Tolkien, *The Fellowship of the Ring*, p. 305.

"Almost brought ruin ... See, there is the fire ..." Tolkien, *The Return of the King*, pp. 797, 731.

"O blessed Meriadoc!" See above, p. 121.

"Can the black riders see?" Tolkien, *The Fellowship of the Ring*, p. 185 (misremembered).

Tom Waits. I am referring to his song "The Black Rider," on his 1993 album of the same title.

Sally Bowles is a character in Christopher Isherwood's so-called Berlin Stories, *Mr. Norris Changes Trains* (1935) and *Goodbye to Berlin* (1939), which were originally intended to form part of a panoramic novel called *The Lost*. These formed the basis of the 1951 play *I Am a Camera,* and of the Broadway musical and subsequent film *Cabaret* (1973). The part of Sally was played in the film by Liza Minelli, who won an Oscar for her performance (as did Bob Fosse for Best Director). Tom Waits's *The Black Rider* album, which originated in a musical review in which Waits collaborated at the Thalia Theatre in Hamburg, is an effective musical nod to Isherwood's murky world of the last days of Weimar.

"That host ... This way and that ..." Tolkien, *The Two Towers,* p. 691.

"Reading Yeats I do not think ..." Lawrence Ferlinghetti, *Pictures of the Gone World,* San Francisco: City Lights Books, poem #26.

American gothic. The allusion is to Grant Wood's celebrated 1930 painting of that title.

Mostly dead sopranos. "Ah, je ris" is from Gounod's opera *Faust,* sung by Adelina Patti on the Electrola album *Adelina Patti,* recorded in December 1905 at her home in Wales. The trifling song of Bizet's is his "Pastorale," sung by Nellie Melba on *The London Recordings,* recorded July 7, 1906. "Ich habe deinen Mund geküsst" is from the closing scene of Richard Strauss's opera *Salome,* sung by the young Ljuba Welitsch on the 1972 HMV Treasury album *Ljuba Welitsch,* recorded in 1944 with the Wiener Rundfunk Orchestra conducted by Lovro von Matacic. Berta Kiurina's record of "Casta diva" from Bellini's *Norma* can be heard on *The Record of Singing,* Vol. 2 (from EMI). "Piangi! Piangi fanciulla" is the duet from Act II of Verdi's *Rigoletto,* sung by Giuseppe de Luca and Amelita Galli-Curci, recorded in New York in 1927 with the Metropolitan Opera orchestra conducted by Giulio Setti. It can be heard on the Lebendige Vergangenheit album *Giuseppe de Luca II.* Claudia Muzio's Edison recordings are collected in the box set *Claudia Muzio Edisons,* issued by Rubini Records in 1981; her later series (including "Addio del passato") are on *Claudia Muzio The Columbia Recording 1934-5,* in the HMV Treasury series. On all these singers, see J. B. Steane's incomparable *The Grand Tradition: Seventy Years of Singing on Record 1900 to 1970,* London: Duckworth, 1974.

"Do you know where you're going to (Theme from Mahogany)?," by M. Masser and G. Goffin, is sung by Diana Ross on her 1976 album *Diana Ross.*

"Je suis le spectre ..." From Hector Berlioz's "Nuits d'été," sung by Maggie Teyte on the album *Mélodies Françaises/French Songs* (EMI Classics/Références, 1994), recorded July 31, 1940. "Laissez-faire Mademoiselle Teyte" is what Debussy is alleged to have said to complaints about the young English singer's renditions of his songs.

"If only I could nudge you ..." Theodore Roethke, "Elegy for Jane, My Student, Thrown by a Horse," in *The Albatross Book of Verse*, p. 619.

"Reviens, reviens ..." Also from Berlioz's "Nuits d'été," sung by Maggie Teyte on *Mélodies Françaises/French Songs*, recorded July 31, 1940.

Maybird. I give these details from my recollections of what my mother and Robin told me. But there are two articles on Maybird, whose name then was Maya, by George Day in the magazine *The Wooden Boat*, nos. 9 (1976) and 16 (1977), recounting its history more fully. My brother-in-law Mr. Darryl Hughes, Maybird's present owner, writes: "G'day. ... You need to be aware that there are some inaccuracies in the George Day articles. From memory the following correct his errors. She was built/launched in 1937. Designed by Fred Shepherd. Oak frames, pitchpine hull planking, teak decks and spruce masts and spars. She was built by John Tyrrell and Sons at South Quay, Arklow, Ireland. Her first owner was Lt Col WCW Hawkes DSO (Indian Army ret'd). I am in constant contact with David Armstrong and his wife who are one half of the crew that sailed her from the UK to New Zealand in 1972–1973. Their children have now all grown up. Interestingly the oldest Mills daughter who is mentioned in the article is now a mid-forties married mum in Auckland and she visited Maybird last year. I am also in touch with the son of Maybird's fourth owner who first saw her in 1949 and spent a summer on her with his father. She was gaff rigged in those days. The Bermudan main sail arrangement was not adopted until 1951 by her fifth owner—Lt Commander John Russell (RNVR). Day's view of her sea keeping qualities is absolutely correct. Robin and I have sailed her in 45 knots of wind with just the jib and the mizzen and really did feel in control of her."

The demonstration of March 17, 1968, outside the United States Embassy at Grosvenor Square in London, was in protest against the Vietnam War. BBC reports estimated the number of demonstrators at over ten thousand. There were over two hundred arrests, and eighty-six people, including police, were treated for injuries.

C. S. Lewis, *The Horse and His Boy* (1954), one of his series of Narnia novels, all of which I read as a child, having won The Sir Malcolm Stewart Prize for English Literature for my essay on *The Lion, the Witch, and the Wardrobe*, the first in the series, in the First Form.

Herat. The photograph that so disturbed me was *not* by James Nachtwey (who has a dramatic 1996 photograph of the ruins of Kabul in the same book), as I remembered and recounted it here. It was Steve McCurry's "Family in their destroyed neighbourhood, Herat, Afghanistan, 1993," in *Magnum Landscape*, New York: Phaidon, 1996, p. 135.

Benenden vowels. Benenden is an exclusive girls' boarding school in Kent, England, founded in 1923. Its alumni include H.R.H. Princess Anne.

"It's no go my honey love ..." Louis MacNiece, "Bagpipe Music," in *The Penguin Book of Contemporary Verse*, edited by Kenneth Allcott, Harmondsworth: Penguin, 1950, p. 165.

"An ax for the frozen sea within me." Franz Kafka, letter to Oskar Pollak, January 27, 1904, in his *Letters to Friends, Family, and Editors,* New York: Schocken, 1977. Kafka was talking of writing.

"You Were Always on My Mind," by Wayne Thompson, Mark James, and Johnny Christopher, is sung by Elvis Presley on the album *Separate Ways* (1973).

Sandringham and Balmoral, named after royal residences in England and Scotland, are neighboring suburbs of Auckland. Hastings, Clive, Khyber Pass, Bombay Hills, Coromandel Peninsular (which recall India) and the Firth of Thames (which disconcertingly vaults the Anglo-Scottish border) are all places in the North Island of New Zealand.

William Shakespeare, *Antony and Cleopatra.* Jane Austen, *Pride and Prejudice. The Beano* and *The Dandy,* English children's comics. *South Pacific,* the 1949 Rogers and Hammerstein musical (Ezio Pinza singing "Some Enchanted Evening"). Daphne du Maurier, *Jamaica Inn.* Cliff Richard, English pop singer.

Neater sweeter maiden. Kipling, "Mandalay," p. 417.

Národní třída, (National Avenue), Náměstí republiky (Republic Square), and Masarykovo nábřeží (Masaryk Embankment, named after Czechoslovakia's first president Tomáš Garrigue Masaryk) are all locations in Prague, where I lived from 1991 to 1993.

Ein Volk, ein Reich, ein Führer (one people, one state, one leader). Nazi slogan.

Coleridge's albatross. In his "The Rhyme of the Ancient Mariner," in Wordsworth and Coleridge, *Lyrical Ballads* (1798).

"So what … Flamenco Sketches." The tracks on Miles Davis's album *Kind of Blue* (1959), possibly the best-selling album in jazz history.

Stormy weather … No one cares. An allusion to Ted Koehler and Harold Arlen's song "Stormy Weather," as sung by Frank Sinatra on the 1959 album *No One Cares,* which had a way cool cover for wannabe teenage existentialists.

"Where Did Our Love Go" was released in the UK in July 1964, *Five by Five* the following month. Bob Dylan's *Blonde on Blonde* came out in May 1966. Steppenwolf's "Born to Be Wild" came out in 1968, which makes this memory problematic but possible; I left home for university that September. My poem "Genèvre" was probably written the previous year, if not earlier.

Ornette Coleman, *New York Is Now!* Blue Note Records, re-released on CD in 1990.

My book *The Coasts of Bohemia: A Czech History* was published by Princeton University Press in 1998. The paper I had wanted to call "Contemporaneities" eventually came out under the title "A Quintessential Czechness" in *Common Knowledge,* vol. 7, no. 2, 1998, pp. 136–164.

"Shadows are falling … Well I've been to London." Bob Dylan, "Not Dark Yet," on the album *Time Out of Mind* (1997).

"Twenty miles out of town." Bob Dylan, "Cold Irons Bound," also on *Time Out of Mind*.

"And we are here as on a darkling plain ..." Matthew Arnold, "Dover Beach."

Magwitch, Pip, Estella, Miss Haversham, etc. Characters in Charles Dickens, *Great Expectations*. Tickler was a rattan cane.

Shelob the spider. Tolkien, *The Two Towers*, book 4, chapter 9.

Mills and Boon. British publisher of romance novels, similar to Harlequin romances in North America.

Darcy, Eliza Bennet. The protagonists of Jane Austen's *Pride and Prejudice*. Pemberley is Darcy's ancestral estate; Elizabeth famously tells her sister Jane that her feelings for Darcy began to change on seeing it. Emma Woodhouse is the heroine of Austen's *Emma*. Mr. Rochester is the male lead in Charlotte Bronte's *Jane Eyre*. Thornfield Hall was his home.

Keith Richards and Mick Jagger, of the Rolling Stones, met as teenagers on Dartford Station, about fifteen miles from the Medway Towns in Kent where I grew up.

Tolkien, *Lord of the Rings*. For Arwen and Aragorn see *The Return of the King*, pp. 1032–1038; for Eowyn and Faramir see *The Return of the King*, pp. 938–944; for Galadriel see *The Fellowship of the Ring*, pp. 356–357; for Luthien see *The Fellowship of the Ring*, pp. 187–190; the appendices, which explain all about Ar-Pharazon and the Fall of Numenor, follow the third volume, *The Return of the King*. The rabbit episode is in *The Two Towers*, pp. 638–641. Isildur's "I shall take this as weregild" is (mis)quoted from *The Fellowship of the Ring*, p. 237.

Rosemary Sutcliffe was a popular British children's author in my childhood. The book of hers I remember best is *The Eagle of the Ninth* (1954; republished by Oxford University Press in 2000).

Poems of the Late T'ang, edited by A. C. Graham, Harmondsworth: Penguin, 1965.

"I was with the Philippine armies ..." *Dr. Who* is a long-running science-fiction saga on British TV, airing early on Saturday evenings from 1963 onwards. Eight actors have so far played the role. This line comes from the story "The Talons of Weng-Chiang," first broadcast in 1977, with Tom Baker as Dr. Who and Louise Jameson as the delectable Leela.

J. R. R. Tolkien, *The Silmarillion*, first published by Allen and Unwin in 1977 (i.e., two years *after* I finished my PhD, but while I was still in Durham on a postdoc). This contains a much longer account of the tale of Luthien and Beren than that related by Aragorn in *The Fellowship of the Ring*.

The desert road is in the central plateau area of the North Island of New Zealand, between Taupo and Waiouru. The three volcanoes are Tongariro, Ngaruahoe, and Ruapehu.

Tess and Jude, etc. Thomas Hardy, *Tess of the d'Urbervilles*, and *Jude the*

Obscure. William Shakespeare, *The Tragedy of Antony and Cleopatra* and *The Winter's Tale*. Set texts for English A Level, along with Chaucer's *Canterbury Tales* and Milton's *Paradise Lost*.

"The soldier's pole is fallen ..." *Antony and Cleopatra*, in William Shakespeare, *The Complete Works*, edited by Stanley Wells and Gary Taylor, Oxford: Clarendon Press, 1986, Act IV, scene 16, p. 1160. My memory has telescoped it. What Shakespeare wrote was: "The soldier's pole is fall'n. Young boys and girls / Are level now with men. The odds is gone, / And there is nothing left remarkable / Beneath the visiting moon."

Crocodile file: walking two-by-two in a column. Blanco: whitening substance used on the belts and gaiters of military uniforms. Boater: straw hat that was part of the King's School uniform. Chapel: compulsory school service every morning, held in Rochester Cathedral. Rugger: the game of rugby.

"My salad days." Shakespeare, *Antony and Cleopatra*, Act I, scene 5, p. 1135. Cleopatra continues: "when I was green in judgment, cold in blood."

Tripped the light fantastic. See John Milton, "L'Allegro," in *L'Allegro and Il Penseroso*, London: John Lane The Bodley Head, 1927, p. 7. There is also an allusion here to Procul Harum's song "A Whiter Shade of Pale," by Keith Reed and Gary Brooker, an enormous hit in England in 1967.

Parotting (Michel) Foucault. Primarily his *Discipline and Punish* (New York: Vintage, 1979)—a book that so often gets dumbed down as merely being about *repression*, despite Foucault's own critique of the gross simplicities of that concept in his *The History of Sexuality*, Vol. 1 (New York: Vintage, 1980).

Atten—shun. Every Thursday afternoon, throughout my senior school years, we dressed up in uniform and played soldiers in the Combined Cadet Force (CCF).

"If you can keep your head when all about you ..." Rudyard Kipling, "If—," in *Rudyard Kipling's Verse*, p. 578. The "undying gayness" is beautifully caught in Marek Kanievska's 1984 film *Another Country*—a thinly disguised portrait of the young Guy Burgess at Eton.

"Half past one ..." T. S. Eliot, "Rhapsody on a Windy Night," p. 26.

The Who released "My Generation" in 1965. Phil Hogan points some gentle fun at much I have recalled here about the era in "Tolkien 'bout my generation," *The Observer*, Sunday January 13, 2002.

The film *Zorba the Greek*, starring Anthony Quinn and Alan Bates, was released in 1964.

"It is old but it is beautiful ..." From "The Sash My Father Wore," an Orange (i.e., Ulster Protestant) marching song. William of Orange ("King Billy") defeated the Irish Catholic forces loyal to the ousted James II on July 1, 1690, at the Battle of the Boyne. These events continue to resonate, sometimes bloodily, in Northern Ireland to this day—as well as in Glasgow, where I lived from 1978 to 1986, a city that has a large population of Irish origin.

"Two books it would be as troubling, now, to own up to as to repudiate." Corrigan, Ramsay, Sayer, *Socialist Construction and Marxist Theory* (1978) and *For Mao* (1979), both published by Macmillan in the UK. *Socialist Construction* was published in the United States by Monthly Review Press, which was how I came to meet Paul Sweezy.

Christina (Kirsty) Larner, author of *Enemies of God* (London: Chatto and Windus, 1981). Kirsty was in her forties when she died. So was Philip Abrams, head of the Department of Sociology at Durham University where I did my PhD from 1972 to 1975, a man for whose support and affection I shall always be profoundly grateful.

"Who would true Valour see ..." From John Bunyan's *Pilgrim's Progress* (1684), subsequently turned into another rousing Anglican hymn.

"Are you or have you ever been a member of the Communist Party?" was a stock question put to those subpoenaed to appear before the House Un-American Activities Committee during Senator Joseph McCarthy's witch-hunts of 1951–54. HUAC pre-dated McCarthy, having blacklisted the Hollywood Ten in 1947. Founded in May 1949, *Monthly Review* is still going strong, with Paul Sweezy as one of its editors.

"Goodbye to my Juan ..." Woody Guthrie, "Plane Crash at Los Gatos (Deportee)." Another song capable of bringing instant tears to my eyes.

Judith Durham was the lead singer of the Australian group The Seekers, whose song "The Carnival Is Over" topped the British charts in October 1965. Dad never had much time for music—Glen Miller and a few other World War II nostalgic memories apart—but he could happily watch Judith all night long. It was a fitting send-off.

"LBJ, LBJ, how many kids ..." A popular chant at anti–Vietnam War rallies in the 1960s.

The Communist Manifesto, Wages, Price and Profit, Capital (in the Moore/Aveling translation). All works by Karl Marx.

Churchill. In the 1945 UK General Election, Clement Attlee's Labour Party trounced Winston Churchill's Conservatives by a landslide. During World War I, as First Lord of the Admiralty, Churchill had masterminded the disastrous Gallipoli landings in the Dardanelles, at which there were enormous losses, notably among ANZAC forces. His use of troops to break a miners' strike in 1910 in Tonypandy in South Wales, when he was home secretary, earned him the undying hatred of the left, which his World War II record has never fully assuaged.

Kim Philby, Guy Burgess, Donald Maclean, Anthony Blunt. British spies for the Soviet Union, all recruited at Cambridge University.

Was he in Spain? I am referring to the Spanish Civil War of 1936–39, and in particular the International Brigades that fought on the Republican side against General Franco's rebels. The books I had in mind here were Ernest Hemingway's *For Whom the Bell Tolls*, George Orwell's *Homage to Catalonia*, and the poetry of W. D. Auden and Steven Spender, all of which I read in my late teens, when the Spanish events were only a generation away (and Franco still ruled Spain). *Poetry of the Thirties,* edited by Robin Skelton (1964), a fine anthology, was reissued by Penguin Books in its Modern Classics series in 2000.

The 1956 Soviet invasion of Hungary led to a mass exodus from the British Communist Party. The Greek civil war raged from 1945 to 1949, with the communist rising eventually being put down with substantial British and American aid. The Yalta meeting between Stalin, Churchill, and Roosevelt in February 1945 left much more unsettled than this suggests, including in regard to the fate of Greece—but I am recalling how George presented it to me then, as a done deal.

"Whereof we cannot speak." Wittgenstein, *Tractatus,* p. 151.

Damien Hirst, the British artist. This is from an interview in the magazine *Dazed and Confused* in September 1997, reprinted in *Star Culture,* New York: Phaidon, 2000, p. 165.

"And when the angels ask me to recall ..." From "I Remember You" by Victor Schertzinger and Johnny Mercer, which was a hit for Frank Ifield in England in 1962.

Edward Hopper noir. I probably had in mind some mélange of "Morning in a City" (1944) and "Woman in the Sun" (1961), reproduced in Levin, *Edward Hopper,* pp. 275 and 298 respectively.

"Tension upon My Toes." The photographs discussed here are from China Hamilton, *Woman,* London: Erotic Print Society, 1999, pp. 121, 123, 125, 127, 133, 135. The titles are his.

Lehmann's *Songs of Vienna,* with Paul Ulanowsky at the piano, are available in the Legendary Performances Series, Columbia Records. They were recorded in New York in July 1941. I cannot track down the Schumann Lieder LP, which is long out of print.

Die Walküre, Act I. Lauritz Melchior, Lotte Lehmann, and Emanuel List, Vienna Philharmonic Orchestra conducted by Bruno Walter, recorded June 20–22, 1935 (*not,* as I remembered, 1938; it could scarcely have been, after the *Anschluss* of March 12–13 of that year!). This is available in the EMI Références series.

"The dark portal ..." Hamilton, *Woman,* p. 11.

"Are you sitting comfortably ..." The ritual opening to the BBC radio program *Listen with Mother,* broadcast every weekday when I was a very small child, actually went like this: "The time is a quarter to two. This is the BBC Light Programme. Are you ready for the music? When it stops, Catherine Edwards will be here to speak to you. [music follows] Are you sitting comfortably? Then I'll begin!" After fifteen minutes of "The Grand Old Duke of York" and "Mary Mary Quite Contrary," the Beeb moved on to *Woman's Hour. Listen with Mother* ran from 1950 to 1982. Started in 1946, *Woman's Hour* is still going, in the 10–11 A.M. slot on BBC Radio 4—the longest-running magazine show in radio history.

Franz Kafka, "In the Penal Colony," in *Selected Short Stories of Franz Kafka*, New York: Modern Library, 1993.

"That perfect curvature ..." Hamilton actually says: "if there is one part of the body of a woman that is a universal magnet, it is her bottom. A bottom can signal so much. It is so often of sheer dimensional beauty, a curving form that touches our soul. ... Bottoms lead us on, tantalize and tease. They are so tempting to touch, so tempting to use. They submit yet they provoke. They are the seat of desire, the object of pleasure and of punishment—so often the union of both these emotional forces" (*Woman*, pp. 10–11.) He offers a spirited, intelligent and lucid refusal to apologize for the sadomasochistic themes of his pictures.

"Real, symbolic, imaginary." The allusion is to the writings of the French psychoanalytic theorist Jacques Lacan, on whom I draw extensively in the essay that follows this memoir. As I noted above, Lacan once owned Courbet's *Origine du monde*.

"Il faut confronter ..." I have not been able to find the source for this. I quote it from memory, from a postcard I used once to have pinned on my office door, but have now lost.

"Thief, thief! Baggins!" Tolkien, *The Fellowship of the Ring*, p. 12.

Spontaneous combustion. The surreal death of Krook, "the Lord Chancellor of the Rag and Bottle shop," in chapter 32 of Charles Dickens, *Bleak House*.

H. Rider Haggard, *King Solomon's Mines* (1885). Smaug is the dragon in J. R. R. Tolkien, *The Hobbit* (1937).

"My precioussss" is how Gollum addressed the ring in Tolkien's books. W. G. Sebald, *Vertigo*, New York: Vintage, 2002; *The Rings of Saturn*.

Daily Telegraph. I could not track the picture down. It may have been in *The Daily Express* or some other British newspaper.

L.S.E. gates. Security gates had been installed in 1968 or 1969 at the London School of Economics as a security measure against student occupations.

On the Angry Brigade, see Martin Bright, "Look Back in Anger," *The Observer*, Sunday February 3, 2002. As Bright observes, it is remarkable just how much these events have been erased from public memory—along with many questions that have yet to be answered.

Baader-Meinhof Gang, German left-wing terrorists active from 1968 to 1977. Most of their leaders, including Andreas Baader and Ulrike Meinhof, were captured in 1972. The German artist Gerhard Richter painted a disturbing and—to me—profoundly moving series of fifteen canvases on the Baader-Meinhof story in 1988, under the title "October 18, 1977" (the date Baader was found shot to death in his prison cell). The one I find most poignant is "Record Player"—a perfectly ordinary phonograph, of the kind we had as students in the 1960s, in which, the police claimed, Baader smuggled in the gun with which he supposedly shot himself. See Robert

Storr, *Gerhard Richter: Forty Years of Painting*, New York: Museum of Modern Art, 2002, where these paintings are reproduced.

Jean-Luc Godard's *British Sounds* was made in 1969 for BBC Weekend Television, which then refused to show it.

Timothy J. Clark's books include *The Absolute Bourgeois, Image of the People, The Painting of Modern Life*, and *Farewell to An Idea: Episodes from the History of Modernism*. He later moved from Harvard to the University of California at Berkeley. He was an early member of the British section of the Situationist International (see next note).

A Situationist Frenchman. Founded in July 1957, the Situationist International has remained a remarkably fertile source of avant-garde political and cultural criticism of capitalist society. The best-known Situationist text is probably Guy Debord's hugely influential *Society of the Spectacle* (1967).

"Keep a clean nose ..." Bob Dylan, "Subterranean Homesick Blues," on the album *Bringing It All Back Home*.

John Le Carré, *Little Drummer Girl*, London: Hodder and Stoughton, 1983.

Doris Lessing, *The Good Terrorist*, London: Cape, 1985.

Brixton, Holloway. Her Majesty's London prisons, for men and women respectively.

"Interpreting it, in various ways." Karl Marx, "Theses on Feuerbach," in his *Collected Works*, Vol. 5 (London: Lawrence and Wishart, 1976), p. 5.

Philosophy leaves the world as it is. See Ludwig Wittgenstein, *Philosophical Investigations*, Oxford: Blackwell, 1974, p. 49.

Dr. Pangloss ... "Il faut cultiver ..." Voltaire, *Candide*. Pangloss is best known for the view that "all is for the best in the best of all possible worlds."

A popular song of the time. "Break On Through to the Other Side," the opening track on The Doors' debut album (also called *The Doors*), released in January 1967.

Jimi Hendrix, Janis Joplin, Jim Morrison (of The Doors), musicians who died young in what might be called lifestyle-related accidents. John F. Kennedy was assassinated on November 22, 1963, his brother Robert in 1968, the same year as Martin Luther King, Jr., who delivered the famous "I have a dream" speech on the steps at the Lincoln Memorial in Washington, D.C., on August 28, 1963. King was shot on April 4, Robert Kennedy on June 5. My Lai was a massacre of over three hundred unarmed Vietnamese civilians by American forces led by Lt. William Calley, on March 16, 1968. Kent State University was the scene of the shooting of several students, four of whom were killed, on May 4, 1970, by National Guard troops called in to quell anti–Vietnam War demonstrations. *Apocalypse Now* is Francis Ford Coppola's 1979 film about the Vietnam War. "Half in love with easeful death" is a line from John Keats's "Ode to a Nightingale" (1819). A morbid set of images, no doubt, far from the "summer of love" we like to remember—but as Susan Sontag tartly observes, "it wasn't the Sixties then" ("Afterword: Thirty Years Later," in her *Against Interpretation and Other Essays,* New York: Picador, 2001).

"Va, pensiero ..." From Giuseppe Verdi's 1842 opera *Nabucco,* quoted here from the website *www.karadar.com/Librettos/verdi_nabucco.html.* The opening line translates as "Go, thought, on golden wings."

Velvet Revolution. The name given by Czechs to the massive but peaceful demonstrations that brought down the communist government in what was then Czechoslovakia in November 1989. The playwright and prominent dissident Václav Havel became president, and Civic Forum won the 1990 elections.

Claudia Muzio. See p. 128. "Ammogliato ..." is from Leoncavallo's opera *Zazà.*

Oh What a Lovely War. Directed by Richard Attenborough, this 1969 film is based on Charles Chilton's 1963 play. The film cast included Laurence Olivier, Ralph Richardson, Maggie Smith, John Gielgud, Michael Redgrave, Jack Hawkins, John Mills, Susannah York, Dirk Bogarde, and Phyllis Calvert. It is remarkable both for its surrealist sensibility and its poignant use of World War I soldiers' songs.

Lindsay Anderson's 1968 film *If* is a tale of revolt in an English public school, starring the young Malcolm McDowell. It takes its title from Kipling's famous poem.

The Falklands War, prompted by Argentina's invasion of the Falkland (or Malvinas) Islands, took place in 1982. William Wyler's *Mrs. Miniver* was a 1942 wartime propaganda film, starring Greer Garson, which won six Oscars. "Once more into the breach ..." are the words Shakespeare puts into the mouth of Henry V at the siege of Harfleur in 1415 (*Henry V,* Act III, scene 1). Sir Francis Drake and Admiral Horatio Lord Nelson are British naval legends. Drake supposedly insisted on finishing his game of bowls before sailing off to engage the Spanish Armada in 1588; Nelson turned a literal blind eye to a signaled order to disengage at the battle of Copenhagen on April 2, 1801, which he went on to win. Pompey is slang for the town of Portsmouth. "Don't Cry for Me Argentina" is from Andrew Lloyd Webber's 1978 musical *Evita.* Ozzie (Osvaldo) Ardiles was an Argentine footballer, who played for the London club Tottenham Hotspur, whose ground is White Hart Lane. The sinking of the *General Belgrano* was a controversial early action during the Falklands War (controversial because the ship was well outside the "exclusion zone" announced by Mrs. Thatcher at the time it was torpedoed by the British). My letter was published in *The Times* on May 7, 1982.

Prince Regent's Pavilion. The Royal Pavilion in Brighton, an ornate mock-oriental residence remodeled from an earlier building by John Nash between 1815 and 1823—the exterior is quasi-Indian, some of the interior *faux*-Chinese—was built for the Prince Regent, the future king George IV. Canute the Great was king of England from 1017 to 1035, as well as of

Denmark, Norway, and part of Sweden; legend has it he set up his throne on the beach and (unsuccessfully) commanded the sea to recede, to demonstrate to fawning courtiers the limitations of all earthly power.

"We'll Hang Out Our Washing ..." Another early World War II English hit, once again sung by Flanagan and Allen.

"What passing bells ..." Wilfred Owen, "Anthem for Doomed Youth," in *The Albatross Book of Verse*, p. 597.

Human capacities perfecting social forms. This is an allusion to Philip Corrigan's book *Social Forms/Human Capacities: Essays in Authority and Difference*, London: Routledge, 1990.

Philip Corrigan and Derek Sayer, *The Great Arch: English State Formation as Cultural Revolution*, Oxford: Blackwell, 1985.

Salvador Dalí, "The Persistence of Memory (Soft Watches)," 1931, reproduced in Robert Descharnes and Gilles Néret, *Salvador Dalí*, Köln: Taschen, 1987, p. 163.

"Listen! You hear the grating roar ..." Matthew Arnold, "Dover Beach."

OH, I DO LIKE TO BE BESIDE
THE SEASIDE

Derek and baby Austin.

Alison, Derek, and Mum
at Birling Gap.

Neil, Alison, and Derek
riding a breaktwater,
possibly at Seaford.

Dad in Germany, 1945.

Dad on honeymoon, Tintagel, Cornwall.

Derek with Grandad.

Mum.

Subject	No. placed	Position	Remarks
ENGLISH	31	30	Disgraceful. He must learn to apply himself to work which does not interest him.
HISTORY	31	5=	
GEOGRAPHY	26	7=	He does not over-strain himself in his pursuit for knowledge in this subject and must guard against becoming complacent.
DIVINITY	31	15	He is capable of holding a higher position than this.
LATIN	31	6	Very satisfactory progress.
FRENCH	31	9	He can do well when he tries.
MATHEMATICS	31	12=	A great improvement; I hope the effort will continue.
PHYSICS or GREEK	26	2=	Very good.
CHEMISTRY	31	1=	Another truly excellent term.
MUSIC			
ART	30	16=	He can produce good work.
Conduct			
Games			
C.C.F.			
Societies, Scouts etc.			
House Master			
Form Master			He is able and can be very irritating.
Head Master			

School report, Lent Term, 1964.

Art class in Satis House.

It was a tricycle I was riding.

Burmese days (Uncle Lou is on the left of the picture).

Derek with Nanny.

IN SEARCH OF A SUBJECT

⊕

*It is not a question of knowing whether I speak of myself in a way
that conforms to what I am, but rather of knowing whether I am
the same as that of which I speak.*

—Jacques Lacan, *Écrits*[1]

*What do our souls seek journeying
on the decks of decayed ships
crowded with sallow women and crying infants
unable to forget themselves, either with the flying fish
or with the stars which the tips of the masts indicate,
grated by gramophone records
bound unwillingly by non-existent pilgrimages
murmuring broken thoughts from foreign tongues?*

—George Seferis, "Mythical Story"[2]

THE FLOATING WORLD

TO SAY THAT THE SUBJECT IS CONSTITUTED IN LANGUAGE is to reject
any notion of an essential subject that exists prior to or outside
language, a subject for whom language serves merely as a vehicle
of expression. If we then ask what can unify the subject—what
can identify a *self* as that which, in Aristotelian logic, is all that is
not not-self, and remains, moreover, the *same* self at different
points in space and time—the answer is fraught with paradox.
For all that permits the location of the subject within language
is the existence of a vacant space, an empty signifier—that me,
myself, I—which is able to signal my uniqueness, my identity, to
the precise extent that the same linguistic space can be occupied
by any and every other human being.[3] We may, of course, attach

143

any number of distinguishing predicates to this empty I, but what is true of the grammatical subject holds equally of anything we might wish to predicate of it. My subjectivity can be signified only through that which is irreducibly not me, myself, I. In language, I share the first person singular space that defines my uniqueness with all others, while outside language my uniqueness cannot be articulated at all. As Wittgenstein said in the *Tractatus,* "the *limits of my language* mean the limits of my world."[4]

An alienation—which Lacan argues is present in the mirror-phase that precedes the infant's acquisition of language, but already entails its identification with and in the *imago* seen in the glass[5]—is thus inherent in the very possibility of any subjectivity that is constituted in language. Hence Jacques Derrida's poignant conundrum: "I have only one language; it is not mine."[6] It is entry into this alien field, the field of language, that alone allows the constitution of "my" self. But to have one's self articulated in and as language, to speak and to be spoken of, is also inescapably to surrender oneself—or, more accurately perhaps, to be surrendered—to language, in all its vicissitudes and vagaries. This primordial estrangement, if we wish to call it that, is the paradox that grounds any subjectivity at all. "I identify myself in language, but only by losing myself in it like an object," Lacan says.[7] Not that this I, *qua* subject, could ever have had any choice in the matter. Lacan's sentence, a sentence that reads oddly if what it states is true, is itself fissured by the same paradox. For it is not that there was an already existent I who decided to enter language, an original self that was ever there to lose. The subject is only *created* in the act of objectification—of "losing oneself" in language—itself. It is found(ed), we might say, in this original loss.

Long before Lacan or Derrida, Emile Durkheim was getting at something similar in his reflections on the idea of the soul. All cultures, he says, recognize "a constitutional duality of human nature"—"man has … everywhere conceived of himself as formed of two radically heterogeneous beings: the body and the soul."[8] Whereas the human body is mortal, "the abode of the soul is elsewhere, and the soul tends ceaselessly to return to it."[9] So universal a belief, he argues, must testify to a fundamental truth about the human condition, which for him is the fact that we do lead "a double existence ... one purely individual and rooted in our organisms, the other social and nothing but an extension of society."[10] What is signified under the name of the soul, he maintains, is the presence of society within us. Here, too, estrangement is constitutive of subjectivity, for society is external to the individual, and at the same time forms his innermost essence— "society commands us because it is exterior and superior to us. ... But as, on the other hand, it is within us and is us, we love and desire it, albeit with a sui generis desire since, whatever we do, society can never be ours in more than a part and dominates us infinitely."[11] Durkheim's subject, just like Lacan's or Derrida's, is congenitally divided, and that division lies at the origin of what it is to be human. "We could not wish to be free of society," he concludes, "without wishing to finish our existence as men."[12]

The Cartesian subject of Enlightenment mythology, the unified, self-conscious *cogito ergo sum*, could nonetheless still perhaps be salvaged so long as language itself continued to be understood as a stable system of meanings, whether that meaning was anchored in a direct relationship between signs and their referents in the real, or at least secured in a rule-governed structure that guaranteed the constancy of the relationship between signifier (sound, image) and signified (concept, idea). In either case we could regard language simply as an object transparent to our intellect, a toolbox of signs of which we remain the masters and can use as we will. But this stability is exactly what so-called poststructuralist theory has put in question. For there is no transcendental signified, no "concept signified in and of itself ... independent of a relationship to language," in which any signifier could ultimately ever be anchored. On the contrary, "every signified is also in the position of a signifier."[13] What is signified in one sign is immediately the signifier of another, so that signification becomes a process of endless deferral.

"The word for moonlight is moonlight,"[14] says a character in Don DeLillo's *The Body Artist*; but the word for moonlight is precisely not (the thing) moonlight, and what the word signifies to me right now, because of a memory of an old song, is pennies in a stream, falling leaves a sycamore, snowfalls in Vermont. Once we admit the capacity of the signifier in this way to *exceed* the signified—to float free from whatever singular reality or concept might once have been believed to pin it down, and instead gesture toward another and another and another signifier in an endlessly ramifying chain—then subjectivity, too, becomes subject to what Derrida calls *différance*.[15] The predicates of the subject slip away into infinity.

Lacan clarifies why, when he likens the signifying chain of language to "rings of a necklace that is a ring in another necklace made of rings." Using a different analogy, he writes that "all discourse is aligned along the several staves of a score," so that "there is, in effect, no signifying chain that does not have, as if attached to the punctuation of each of its units, a whole articulation of relevant contexts suspended 'vertically,' as it were, from that point."[16] Meaning proliferates—endlessly, and from every point. The problem is not its absence but its superfluity. What we have here is a chain of

> syntheses and referrals which forbid at any moment, or in any sense, that a simple element be *present* in and of itself, referring only to itself. Whether in the order of spoken or written discourse, no element can function as a sign without referring to another element which itself is not simply present. This interweaving results in each "element" ... being constituted on the basis of the trace within it of the other elements of the chain. ... This interweaving, this textile, is the *text* produced only in the transformation of another text. Nothing, neither among the elements nor within the system, is anywhere either simply present or absent. There are only, everywhere, differences and traces of differences.[17]

Where is the I in this necklace-chain, this textile, this text, if not everywhere—carried onward wherever the *glissade* of signification leads—and yet, *essentially*, nowhere?

The ambiguity Foucault so often plays upon when discussing the subject is thus already pre-given in its constitution in language, prior to any particular social disciplinary regime.[18] To be a subject is always (also) to be a subject of and subject to, at least, the slippages of language itself. It is ipso facto, I would argue, also to be a subject of, and subject to, that world which Wittgenstein says my language *is*, and Peter Winch (in *The Idea of a Social Science*) explicates as the social relations that give our language games their meaning.[19] Hearing Herb Alpert sing "This Guy's in Love with You," I feel mushy—an experience that would be inconceivable outside of a very particular (social, historical) subject-formation. The equally particular sexual fantasies that have threaded this memoir would be equally incomprehensible had I not been raised in an English public school—where *getting the cane* had already been invested with all the attributes of sacredness, ripe for perversion. "The sacred object inspires us, if not with fear, at least with respect that keeps us at a distance; at the same time it is an object of love and aspiration that we are drawn towards," writes Durkheim.[20] If I nonetheless do not go on from here to embrace a sociological determinism—to dissolve the subject entirely into structure—it is not because I wish to cling onto the humanistic conception of the unified subject who exercises sovereign free will. It is because language, at least if poststructuralist theorists are right, does not *itself* possess any determinate, centered structure. This realization threatens to undermine the entire basis upon which sociology has been classically founded, bounded as the discipline is by a Cartesian subject (the rational actor) at one pole, and a structuralist conception of the object (society) at the other. Both of these are in jeopardy if both the social world itself, and any language we might use to talk about it, are made up of sliding signifiers.

There is no longer any Archimedean point, whether in the world outside language, or in the presumed consistency of the relation between signifier and signified in language itself, to anchor the subjects that are constituted within language. The only certainty we have is the inevitability of *différance*. To say that the subject is constituted in language, then, is above all to say, with Derrida, that:

> There is no subject who is agent, author, and master of *différance* ... [that] the subject, and first of all the conscious and speaking subject, depends upon the system of differences and the movement of *différance*, that the subject is not present, nor above all present to itself before *différance*, that the subject is constituted only in being divided from itself, in becoming space, in temporizing, in deferral. ...[21]

What we are accustomed to think of as the self does not *contain* the subject. As Lacan puts it, "man's ego can never be reduced to his experienced identity," for "the subject goes far beyond what is experienced 'subjectively' by the individual."[22]

The materials in and out of which subjectivity is fashioned are labile, fluid, slippery, and treacherous—shifting markers that are always deferring beyond the self, always pointing somewhere else, toward some otherness that perpetually threatens to undo who we (think we) are. The subject is a moveable feast, always gesturing, or perhaps we should say—for active and passive voices slip into one another here, as agency becomes less than clear— always gestured, elsewhere.

DRAWING FROM MEMORY

IDENTITY, FROM THIS POINT OF VIEW, becomes an extraordinarily problematic category—much as it might form both the intuitive basis of our everyday perceptions of ourselves, and the epistemological bedrock of our scientific knowledge of others, whose cultures we ethnograph, whose social welfare we measure, whose histories we write. If the foregoing arguments, which are after all no more than the commonplaces of the poststructuralist revolution that has swept the humanities in the last three decades, hold water, then identity—whether we are speaking of an individual or of a collective (a race, a class, a gender, a nation, a society)[23]—*cannot* be what we usually imagine it to be; at least, not so long as we continue to equate identity with the subject, and reduce the subject to his, her, or its identity.

According to *The Oxford English Dictionary*, identity is:

1. The quality or condition of being the same in substance, composition, nature, properties, or in particular qualities under consideration; absolute or essential sameness; oneness. 2. The sameness of a person or thing at all times or in all circumstances; the condition or fact that a person or thing is itself and not something else; individuality, personality.

But if the subject is constituted in language, identity, in any of these senses, is the one quality it is manifestly incapable of possessing. The aporia that constitutes subjectivity is precisely that the subject can be itself, only insofar as it is identified in and as something *other*; while being subject to all the *différance* of language, it cannot exhibit *sameness* in substance, composition, nature, and properties, or at all times and in all circumstances. The subject is never "present in and of itself, referring only to itself"—"absolute or essential sameness, oneness," is something that is congenitally beyond it. To adapt Baudelaire, the medium, in which the subject has its being, is *"le transitoire, le fugitif, le contingent."*

When Baudelaire famously used this formulation to describe "modernity," he was not referring, as most social theorists who have since taken up the term do, to a supposed stage of human thought or history. He was describing *any* temporal present, the present as present, in its intrinsic fleetingness, with reference to the necessity for the artist, as he saw it, "to extract the eternal from the ephemeral."[24] "Every old-time painter," he says, "had his own modernity."[25] Baudelaire's painter of modern life, Monsieur G., returning from a day of busy *flâneurie* to record images of what he has seen, may serve us as a provisional metaphor for the ways in which the transitory, fugitive, and contingent materials out of which subjectivity is constituted are parlayed into (and in turn effaced by) identity. The relation of what, for want of a better word, we may call the real, and the various *imagos* in which—always after the fact[26]—we seek to (re)capture it, to pin it down, is the crux of the matter.

By day, G. walks the streets of Paris, animated by "a fatal and irresistible passion" for life. Baudelaire compares G's openness to the world, "even in the apparently most trivial things," to that of a convalescent "recently returned from the shades of death," who "delightedly breathes in all the germs and odors of life."[27] Convalescence, Baudelaire goes on, "is a sort of return to childhood": "for the child everything is new; he is always exhilarated." He relates a friend's childhood memory of watching his father dressing, as he gazed "in wonderment mixed with delight, at the muscles of the arms, the graduated shades of pink and yellow in the skin, and the bluish network of veins."[28] G. is a "child-man," "the perfect spectator," "an I insatiably eager for the not-I."[29] He walks the city streets long into the evening, "the last person remaining wherever light shines, poetry thunders, life teems, music throbs."[30] Only then does G. take up his pencil, pen, and brush, and begin to draw—"eager, violent, busy," says Baudelaire, "as if he feared that his images might escape him."[31]

And what does G. draw—or better, *how* does he draw? First, Baudelaire tells us, "he draws from memory, not from a model," for such artists, "long accustomed to using their memory and to filling it with images, find, when confronted with the model and its multiplicity of detail, that their chief faculty is disturbed and, as it were, paralysed." There is a perpetual struggle between "the will to see everything and forget nothing, and the memorizing faculty, which has become accustomed actively to absorb general colors, silhouettes, and all the arabesques of contour." G. does not attempt to give "impartial heed to all details" (which Baudelaire tellingly likens to "an insurgent mob"), but exerts, rather, "a resurrective, evocative memory, which bids every object: 'Lazarus, arise!'" This acknowledges that what the artist draws has always already *passed away.*

The second thing Baudelaire stresses about G's method is "a fiery exhilaration of the pencil and brush, almost resembling an outburst of mania. It is the fear of not being fast enough, of letting the phantom escape before its essence has been distilled and captured. ..." The corpse has now become a ghost, haunting the artist until he can exorcise it by capturing its *imago.* Beginning with light pencil strokes, G. adds wash-tints, "vague masses of faint color at first, but later on retouched and loaded with colors successively more intense. Only at the last moment are the outlines of the various objects definitely marked in ink." He finally chooses just a few sketches from the many available to him, "and makes greater or lesser additions to their intensity, darkening the shades and progressively brightening the highlights."[32] And thus we arrive at *essence.* Karl Marx had some sharp things to say about such moonshining a century and a half ago, in *The Holy Family.* He called it "the mystery of speculative construction."[33]

In a not dissimilar way, the photographer Ansel Adams, using an aperture setting that yields a depth of field that far exceeds the perceptual capabilities of the human eye, and manipulating the grayscale to achieve maximum contrast, fixed the Rocky Mountains in our minds in indelible images of what we could never see. Dorothea Lange effected a comparable *trompe l'oeil* when she removed an intrusive thumb, an unruly detail that detracted from the symmetry of the composition, from the negative of her famous 1936 photograph "Migrant Mother," in the process creating what is perhaps the most iconic of all visual images of the Great Depression.[34] This "straight photography," as its proponents called it, achieves its illusion of immediate identity with the real by expunging every trace of the real that might clutter up the photograph and dilute its power to speak. The lucidity of these images, as of any sign, is founded in *différance*—they can represent the real, in the double sense of standing in for it and presenting it anew, because and to the extent that they depart from it.

Speaking of his own photographic practice, Edward Weston gives the game away when he claims that the camera "enables [the photographer] to reveal the essence of what lies before his lens with such clear insight that the beholder may find the re-created image more real and comprehensible than the actual object."[35] As Siegfried Kracauer remarked, Weston—whose photographs are often stunningly beautiful in their stark simplicity, a high point of modernist aesthetics—"often indulges in wrestling abstract compositions from nature."[36] This same *différance* also means that the image perpetually gestures elsewhere. "Migrant Mother," for instance, evokes not only other photographic images from the dirty thirties like Walker Evans's series *Let Us Now Praise Famous Men*,[37] but the entire literature of Madonna and Child painting, semantically coupling poverty and purity in a way that would have been impossible had not the living subject, Florence Thompson, stepped through the lens of Lange's camera and out into the realm of the signifier. Ansel Adams's Rockies, likewise, may conjure up other photographed landscapes, or recall other things that have come to signify an imagined America, like, say, Edward Hopper's painting "Gas," which in turn may direct our mind to "American Gothic" or "Christina's World"[38]—or not. But they will always evoke something, which is other than the Rocky Mountains themselves, and the trace of that something other is integral to their ability to represent that landscape—and in turn, to inform the way that we picture and come to remember it—at all.

What I wish to draw attention to here is the process of abstraction through which the remembered remains of the real are resurrected as graven images. We might call it a *fixation*, bearing

in mind both the photographic and the psychoanalytic reso-
nances of the term. Either way, the flux of life—*le transitoire, le
fugitif, le contingent*—is arrested, whether in a moment of *temps
perdu* frozen on photo-sensitive paper, or in an obsessive psycho-
logical return of the ever-same. For let us be clear that there is
nothing in the real to which the image *corresponds*; it *represents*
a reality that has already passed away. The image can stand in for
this reality not because it resembles it or reproduces it, but
because it has supplanted it.

Summing up Monsieur G's extraction of "the eternal from
the ephemeral," Baudelaire expresses it like this:

> And objects are reborn upon the paper, true to life and more
> than true to life, beautiful and more than beautiful, strange
> and endowed with an enthusiastic vitality, like the soul of
> their author. *Out of nature has been distilled fantasy.* All the
> stuffs with which memory is encumbered are classified and
> arranged in order, are harmonized and subjected to that com-
> pulsory formalization which results from a childish percep-
> tiveness—that is to say, a perceptiveness acute and magical by
> reason of its simplicity![39]

Nietzsche put the same idea more succinctly: "To experience a
thing as beautiful means: to experience it necessarily wrongly."[40]

Identity, I want to suggest, is fabricated out of *différance* by
an analogous magic. It is a representation of the subject, constructed wholly in the realm of the imaginary; a representation
founded in every bit as violent an abstraction, as radical a simplification, as Monsieur G., Adams, Lange, or Weston wreak on
their respective subjects. Identity is not the living being of the
subject, but its *imago*, forged (in both senses of the word) out of
the *memory* of what once was but no longer is; and it is in the
guise of this counterfeit that the subject enters the symbolic
register of society.

We could express this in the simple, if enigmatic formula that I arrived at in my memoir: *identity = being in denial.*

FREUDIAN SLIP

As with many of what I am supposed to imagine are "my" ideas, I did not (consciously, deliberately, actively) "think up" this formula. It came to me, not entirely unbidden, since it sprung out of the associative *glissade* of another signifying chain (the last stanza of Philip Larkin's "High Windows," the song "Blue Skies," René Magritte's painting "The False Mirror," and thence to the visual pun in his "La Condition Humaine"). But it was unexpected nonetheless—a found object. This is therefore, perhaps, an appropriate occasion to ask in passing, also with Nietzsche, who (or what) is the subject of thought—for to say *cogito* here seems a disingenuous account of how this formulation sprang to my mind, unless we acknowledge that the I *who thinks* is someone (or something) other than the I who recognizes in the passing thought an idea worth seizing.[41] As Lacan once put it, teasing us with all the duplicity of language to reconsider that easy *cogito ergo sum,* "I think where I am not, therefore I am where I do not think."[42]

We do, as it happens, have a template for thinking the Alice-in-Wonderland (or more accurately, perhaps, Through-the-Looking-Glass) logic of identity, though it is not one to which I am wholly wedded.[43] This is the familiar Freudian topography of the id, the ego, and the superego—or to use Freud's own more down-to-earth German, whose literal English translation I prefer here, the It (*es*), the I (*Ich*), and the Over-I (*Über-Ich*). The baroque absurdity of this triptych bears pondering. For the trifurcation of the subject is the direct consequence of the fact that identity can be achieved only in the realm of the imaginary. Having been expelled from the imagined I, the *différance* that constitutes the subject in language eternally returns in the sub-versions of the It, which is the place where the signifiers continue to play, but is now no longer recognizable by the ego as a part of the self. *It* manifests the absent presence of *différance* in the cryptic disturbances of the joke, the slip of the tongue, the dream, the symptoms of an original non-identity that may have been denied, but cannot finally be overcome. The self, meantime, has nonetheless still to be reconciled with the symbolic order, and this can now be conceived only in the form of the superego standing menacingly outside, over and above the supposedly self-contained I to which the subject, in its infinite variety, has been reduced.

The joke is undoubtedly on the self, and it is a masterpiece of Bretonian black humor.[44] The imaginary overcoming of the original estrangement that accompanies the constitution of the subject in language (if, as I said, we want to call it that) is purchased at the exorbitant price of a further alienation. Its sign is the Freudian trinity itself, in which another mythological triad, one fundamental to classical sociology, is prefigured—the Tweedledum and Tweedledee of Culture (or Society) and Nature, the hammer and anvil between which the sovereign Individual must negotiate his way home like Odysseus skirting Scylla and Charybdis, wavering between the devil and the deep blue sea. This synthesis of identity is not the resolution of a contradiction, but merely its displacement. As Derrida remarks in another context, "if there were a definition of *différance*, it would be precisely the limit, the interruption, the destruction of the Hegelian *relève* [*Aufhebung* or sublation] *wherever* it operates."[45] The imaginary *relève* that synthesizes the self in an *imago* in and with which it identifies (itself) effects and conceals a radical fissuring of the subject, which renders its being in *différance* unrecognizable. Identity is sublimation, to use Freud's term, not sublation—and it everywhere leaves behind it subliminal traces of the *différance* it denies.

I long wondered why, at the beginning of *Nadja*, André Breton answers his question "Who am I?" with another question, "Whom do I haunt?"[46]—since an orthodox Freudian view of the unconscious, as the archaic repository of unresolved complexes, sublimated drives, and repressed instincts, would lead us to expect him rather to ask "By whom am I haunted?" But Breton's question is the right one. For there is a long-departed I, of a kind, whose specter does haunt the ego of the Freudian triptych, in exactly the same way that the ghosts of the departed real haunt the images confected by Baudelaire's nighttime Monsieur G. The ghost is that of the lost subject found(ed) in language, the subject who has no identity, the subject whose being is subject to the play of the signifier. This is what (in Breton's words) "I must have ceased to be in order to be *who* I am," and whose fixation in an *imago* has the for him paradoxical consequence of "mak[ing] me, still alive, play a ghostly part."[47] We are reminded here of Freud's deceptively simple words, which so impacted later on Jacques Lacan: *Wo es war, soll Ich werden*— where It (the unconscious) was, I must become.[48]

Breton concludes that "this sense of myself ... seems inadequate only insofar as it presupposes myself, arbitrarily preferring a completed image of my mind, which need not be reconciled with time, and insofar as it implies—within this same time—an idea of irreparable loss, of punishment, of a fall whose lack of moral basis is, as I see it, indisputable."[49] The convolutions of his language here mark the complexity of that of which he is attempting to speak.

Thinking about what that "irreparable loss" might be—in the real time to which Breton alludes, with which the image of the self does not need to be reconciled—let us recall for a moment the daytime Monsieur G., Baudelaire's irrepressible *flâneur*. The being of this child-man actually consists of perpetually trying to (sub)merge his self into something else. He is "an I insatiably eager for the not-I"—and it is this *dissolution* of identity, according to Baudelaire, that gives G's eye its keenness:

The masses are his domain, as the air is the bird's and the sea the fish's. His passion is his profession—that of wedding himself to the masses. To the perfect spectator, the impassioned observer, it is an immense joy to make his domicile among numbers, amidst fluctuation and movement, amidst the fugitive and the infinite. To be away from home, and yet to feel at home; to behold the world, to be in the midst of the world, and yet to remain hidden from the world ...

The observer is a prince who always rejoices in his incognito. ... He may also be compared to a mirror as huge as the masses themselves; to a kaleidoscope endowed with awareness, which at each of its movements reproduces the multiplicity of life and the restless grace of all life's elements.[50]

In the daytime, in real time, G's being is impelled by desire, and the object of that desire is always what is other. He does not want to possess that other, so much as lose himself in it; and in that losing he finds himself mirrored in the endlessly moving kaleidoscope of the multiplicity that surrounds him, rediscovered moment by moment, ever renewed. The slogan that defines this subjectivity would have to be *incognito ergo sum*—I am insofar as I am not my self.

Why I think the formula identity = being in denial fortuitous, is because of the duality of meanings that it condenses. It may be taken to mean either that identity is the denial of being, or that identity is being-in-denial, in the psychoanalytic sense of suppressing an unacceptable truth. I intend to convey both. What, above all, the fixation of the flux of being in an *imago* of identity denies, but at the same time enables us to live in denial of, is the dispersal of the subject from which we began; the non-identity that follows from its original constitution in language, of which Baudelaire's prince rejoicing in his incognito furnishes a suggestive model. This specious *relève* is no small accomplishment—to immobilize the *différance* of subjectivity in the singularity of identity is a deception of breathtaking proportions. It comes, however, at a cost. For what it requires is nothing less than that

we treat the flux of the real as imaginary, in order to treat the
fixation of the imaginary as real.

It should not, therefore, surprise us to discover that this self
is a precarious construct, as anything founded in denial ultimately must be. Identity is the flimsiest of garments, ever liable to
unravel, unpicking along every ill-stitched seam. Albert Camus
beautifully captures a chance moment where it begins, for no
apparent reason, to come apart, in his novella *The Fall*:

> I had gone up on the Pont des Arts, deserted at that hour, to
> look at the river that could hardly be made out now night had
> come. Facing the statue of the Vert-Galant, I dominated the
> island. I felt rising within me a vast feeling of power and—I
> don't know how to express it—of completion, which cheered
> my heart. I straightened up and was about to light a cigarette,
> the cigarette of satisfaction, when, at that very moment, a laugh
> burst out behind me. Taken by surprise, I suddenly wheeled
> around; there was no one there. I stepped to the railing; no
> barge or boat. I turned back toward the island and, again, heard
> the laughter behind me, a little farther off as if it were going
> downstream. I stood there motionless. The sound of the laugh-
> ter was decreasing, but I could still hear it distinctly behind me,
> come from nowhere unless from the water. At the same time I
> was aware of the rapid beating of my heart. Please don't misun-
> derstand me; there was nothing mysterious about that laugh; it
> was a good, hearty, almost friendly laugh, which re-established
> the proper proportions. Soon I heard nothing more, anyway. I
> returned to the quays, went up the rue Dauphine, bought some
> cigarettes I didn't need at all. I was dazed and had trouble
> breathing. That evening I rang up a friend, who wasn't at home.
> I was hesitating about going out when, suddenly, I heard laugh-
> ter under my windows. I opened them. On the sidewalk, in fact,
> some youths were loudly saying good night. I shrugged my
> shoulders as I closed the windows; after all, I had a brief to

study. I went into the bathroom to drink a glass of water. My reflection was smiling in the mirror, but it seemed to me that my smile was double....[51]

The unexpected, a laugh coming out of nowhere, has opened up a gap between the lawyer and his *imago*, whose identity he for the first time begins to doubt. He will never be able to close that gap again.

DAYDREAM BELIEVER

I LONG AGO FIRST MISHEARD, AND THEN MISREMEMBERED, the chorus of The Monkees' song "Daydream Believer" as "Cheer up sleepy G.," instead of "Cheer up sleepy Jean"; which is why, I suppose, it unfailingly comes to mind in connection with Baudelaire and "The Painter of Modern Life." This connection is absurd from any logical point of view; but there is no reason to suppose that the chains of association through which memory works operate according to the laws of Aristotelian logic.

I want to suggest that it is in memory, above all, that the fixation of identity in an *imago* takes place. What we know as the self is always recollected, forever being put together (again), re-membered, after the fact. What Baudelaire calls "the memorizing faculty" is pivotal to maintenance of identity, which would be unthinkable without it. We say of someone who has lost his memory, that he has forgotten who he is (and not, as we should say if we were to be logical about it, who *he was*). But this is not the whole story. Because of its ineradicable dependency upon *différance*, upon signifiers that float (away), memory always also remains a locus of potential disintegration. *Lieux de memoire*[52] are treacherous places, because the condensation that fixes them as *points de capiton* for the imagined *I* may always unravel, displacing them to become signifiers of something else. A signifier on the loose may lead us God knows where, and sometimes, like that laugh on the Pont des Arts, it may take us places where the I is unable any longer to recognize what it sees in the mirror as itself. This is the point of my "Daydream Believer" example, trivial as it may be. It is in the quotidian quality of its illogicality that this improbable displacement is so interesting—for it reveals the surreality, to come back to André Breton, that always lurks at the heart of what we imagine to be the real—the play of *différance*, of which we can never finally be rid.

At the start of *The Book of Laughter and Forgetting*, Milan Kundera presents us with a powerful image of erasure of memory. In a photograph that circulated widely in communist Czechoslovakia, the fur hat on Party leader Klement Gottwald's head was the only trace that remained of one-time Foreign Minister Vlado Clementis after the censors' airbrushes had done a Dorothea Lange on the visual record of the communist coup d'état of February 1948. Clementis, who had been standing beside Gottwald when the picture was taken, was executed following the Slánský show trial in December 1952. The trace remains in the photograph, fortuitously, only because it had started to snow, and Clementis removed the hat from his own head and put it on Gottwald's before the latter harangued the masses from the balcony of the Kinský Palace in Prague's Old Town Square. This grotesque anecdote introduces what is perhaps the most quoted—and arguably the most misunderstood—sentence Kundera ever wrote: "It is 1971, and Mirek says that the struggle of man against power is the struggle of memory against forgetting."[53]

A character in Ivan Klíma's *Love and Garbage* is another Czech who laments that "in our country, everything is forever being remade: beliefs, buildings, and street names. Sometimes the progress of time is concealed and at others feigned, so long as nothing remains as real and truthful testimony."[54] Klíma confronts us with the vertiginous terror of a perpetual amnesia, in which there is no longer anything real to confirm the truth of the memories in which identity is anchored, only an endless parade of transparent fictions that are imposed retrospectively and updated every day. History, here, becomes palpably an artifact of the present, just like in the Czech joke of the period:

"The future is certain, comrades! Only the past is unpredictable." As with the repeatedly revised back-copies of the newspapers in George Orwell's *Nineteen Eighty-Four,* successive rewritings have put the reality of what has gone before beyond recovery.[55] The original, if we may speak of such a thing, is irretrievably lost. This produces a peculiar pathos. Klíma's characters know very well that they live in a world of simulacra, but no longer have any means of telling good copies from bad—not unlike myself, revisiting the beach at Seaford for the first time in forty years in the summer of 2001, and having no way of knowing whether the breakwaters I so vividly remembered had been washed away by the tide in the years in between, or had always been figments of my imagination, inserted from elsewhere into my picture of Seaford at some later date, the better to remember it.

This pathos, however, is entirely dependent upon our acceptance of the notion that behind the never-ending erasures there exists some *authentic* primal identity whose truth reposes in the memory of realities that have been washed away by the tide of history; that we do not live in a Baudrillardian world.[56] It is this same postulate of authenticity that makes memory a poignant locus of resistance for Kundera's Mirek, defending his human integrity in the teeth of the manifest fabrications of power. But Kundera himself is much less sentimental than his hero—or than Ivan Klíma. In *The Art of the Novel,* he warns us against taking Mirek's pronouncement as "the book's message."[57] The truth, he says, is far more complicated—and less heroic. The message is not the familiar Orwellian theme: "The originality of Mirek's story lay somewhere else entirely. This Mirek who is struggling with all his might to make sure he is not forgotten (he and his friends and their political battle) is at the same time doing his utmost to make people forget another person (his ex-mistress, whom he's ashamed of)."[58]

In his later book of essays *Testaments Betrayed,* Kundera goes still further. Not only does he abandon Mirek's comforting equations of humanity = remembering, and power = forgetting. He confounds the very opposition of memory and forgetting from which they draw their emotional force, generalizing Mirek's apparent personal duplicity into an existential condition. Much more than intention, or bad faith, are at issue here. I shall quote the relevant passage at length, since it is basic to my argument:

> We are resigned to losing the concreteness of the present. We immediately transform the present moment into its abstraction. We need only recount an episode we experienced a few hours ago: the dialogue contracts to a brief summary, the setting to a few general features. This applies to even the strongest memories, which affect the mind deeply, like a trauma: we are so dazzled by their potency that we don't realize how schematic and meager their content is.
>
> When we study, discuss, analyse a reality, we analyse it as it appears in our mind, in our memory. We know reality only in the past tense. We do not know it as it is in the present, in the moment when it's happening, when it is. The present moment is unlike the memory of it. Remembering is not the negative of forgetting. Remembering is a form of forgetting.
>
> We can assiduously keep a diary and note every event. Rereading the entries one day, we will see that they cannot evoke a single concrete image. And still worse: that the imagination is unable to help our memories along and reconstruct what has been forgotten. The present—the concreteness of the present—as a phenomenon to consider, as a structure, is for us an unknown planet; so that we can neither hold on to it in our memory nor reconstruct it through imagination. We die without knowing what we have lived.[59]

As Kundera presents it, the relation between the reality of the present in which we live, and the memories in which we recollect it, is exactly the relation of Baudelaire's daytime and nighttime Monsieur G. The only difference is Kundera's melancholy, his nostalgia for the *temps perdu* that has gone beyond recall; but

Baudelaire, after all, was concerned not with the truth of the reality that was lost but with the beauty of the fantasy that was reborn from it, forever immortalized in a work of art. (Another signifying chain beckons here: art = artifice = artificial = synthetic = Hegel's *faux-relève:* an *imitation.*) As Maurice Blanchot remarks—"And artists who exile themselves in the illusion of images, isn't it their task to idealize beings, to elevate them to their disembodied resemblance?"[60]

For those attracted to the defiant humanism expressed in Mirek's declaration, what Kundera has to say here is profoundly disturbing—every bit as disturbing, in fact, as we might expect of the author of a vicious short story, "The Hitchhiking Game," in which the presumption of identity itself is pitilessly deconstructed. A young girl, having stripped naked and wiggled obscenely on a table in a cheap hotel room, playing the two-bit whore for her boyfriend, is left in tears, repeating over and over, as she lies beside him afterwards in the bed, "I'm me, I'm me....'"

> The young man was silent, he didn't move, and he was aware of the sad emptiness of the girl's assertion, in which the unknown was defined by the same unknown.
>
> And the girl soon passed from sobbing to loud crying and went on endlessly repeating this pitiful tautology: "I'm me, I'm me, I'm me...."[61]

This tautology ought to give us pause, in the present context. For what it reveals is the void, the vacancy, the lack, which the assumption of identity with an *imago* of the self both denies and enables us to live in denial of—and which has unexpectedly opened up again in the space created by what started out as a titillating game, just as it did for the successful liberal lawyer in Camus' *The Fall* at that moment when he stopped to light his self-satisfied cigarette on the Pont des Arts.

Asked in an interview reproduced in *The Art of the Novel* about the significance of this story, Kundera replied with a reference to another of his books:

In *The Unbearable Lightness of Being,* Tereza is staring at herself in the mirror. She wonders what would happen if her nose were to grow a millimetre longer every day. How much time would it take for her face to become unrecognizable? And if her face no longer looked like Tereza, would Tereza still be Tereza? Where does the self begin and end? You see: Not wonder at the immeasurability of the soul; rather, wonder at the uncertain nature of the self and its identity.[62]

This image of finding in a mirror a way out of the existential tautology of defining an unknown by the same unknown recurs in Lacan, Baudelaire, Camus, and now Kundera. He employs the same figure in *The Art of the Novel* when discussing kitsch, which he defines as "the need to gaze into the mirror of the beautifying lie and be moved to tears of gratification at one's own reflection."[63] The archetype for such identification, of course, is Narcissus, fixated by his reflection in a pool. Could we then go so far as to say: identity is—necessarily—a species of kitsch? And that kitsch, therefore, is the very stuff of any organized social existence?

It is far too easy simply to read the specter of amnesia in modern Czech fiction politically, as an indictment of communism's flagrant distortions of history, which on one level—even for Milan Kundera[64]—it plainly is. As Zdeněk Nejedlý, Czechoslovakia's cultural plenipotentiary for a decade after 1948, expressed it, with greater honesty than he perhaps intended, "To us, history is not the dead past, indeed *it is not the past at all,* it is an ever-living part of the present too."[65] A *longue durée* perspective might go further, and detect in the repeated cycles of remembering and forgetting that are so characteristic of Czech history an instability of identity endemic to this uneasy center of Europe.[66] I want, however, to offer a more radical reading here. This is that the amnesia described by these writers is not some uniquely Czech or communist aberration, but provides an occasion for reflection on what Kundera calls "an existential situation."[67] The absurdities of modern Czech experience merely make manifest a more general truth. For when and where, we might ask, was it ever *not* the case that "beliefs, buildings, and street names" were being remade—with all the attendant vertigo that Klíma implies?[68] When was the original *not* always already lost at the point where it became a memory? The problem, as I see it, is rather to explain how the improbable fiction of identity, of an essential, authentic oneness, a simple *presence* that exists outside of the metamorphoses of time—to recall André Breton's depiction of that *imago* whom he haunts—could ever have been sustained in the face of the reality of *le transitoire, le fugitif, le contingent* at all.

It is precisely here that memory works its Baudelairean magic, distilling fantasy out of the ghosts of the real. We can experience ourselves as possessing identity across space and time, only because our memory provides us with the means of continually *recollecting* ourselves in the imagined space of a past that is ever-present. It is able to do this, however, to the precise extent that memory indeed *is* a form of forgetting. This is far more than simply a question of selectivity, partiality, or repression; of what we like, or don't like, to remember—though it is doubtless that as well (Lacan wryly observes that "the amnesia of repression is one of the liveliest forms of memory").[69] The fundamental issue is of the *différance* between *all* memory and what it purports to be a memory of—and what this *différance,* in its detachment of signifier and signified, makes possible.

Memory operates entirely in the register of the symbolic, not of the real. Despite their sometimes astonishing tactility, our memories are not the *things* we remember (as we habitually, and tellingly, refer to them, occluding words and things and denying the *différance* that always separates them), any more than history is the past or the word for moonlight is moonlight. The things we remember have always, already, and without exception, *passed away.* Like Clementis. What we call their memory is merely a trace, existing wholly in the realm of the signifier, which has always already gone through that transformative alchemy so well described by Kundera and Baudelaire. It is liable to be transmuted again—and again, and again. "Your first memory," explains the heroine of Julian Barnes's *England, England,*

> wasn't something like your first bra, or your first friend, or your first kiss, or your first fuck, or your first marriage, or your first child, or the death of your first parent, or your first sudden sense of the lancing hopelessness of the human condition—it wasn't like any of that. It wasn't a solid, seizable thing, which time, in its plodding, humorous way might decorate down the years with fanciful detail—a gauzy swirl of mist, a thundercloud, a coronet—but could never expunge. A memory was by definition not a thing, it was ... a memory. A memory now of a memory a bit earlier of a memory before that of a memory way back when.[70]

Memories stand in the same relation to the experiences that gave rise to them as images do to the real: they do not correspond to reality, they represent (which is to say, replace) it, and what enables them to do so is *différance*. Vlado Clementis could be airbrushed out of the photograph, and whatever that image might have conjured up in Czech minds, only because the photograph was *not* identical with the reality it depicted—only because Clementis himself had already become a corpse, dangling at the end of a hangman's rope.

Two years after Mirek made his touching pronouncement about memory and resistance, the image of Vlado Clementis was resurrected on a Czechoslovak postage stamp in the guise of a "Fighter against Nazism and Fascism during the Occupation" of 1939–45, in which avatar he blanketed the country. His dates of birth and death were given, but there was nothing to connect the latter with the Slánský trial of the same year. And why should we expect there to be? This resurrection is no less grotesque than the original erasure. But both illustrate the same point. As with all phenomena of memory, Clementis was no longer a solid, seizable thing. His life and death had long since turned into signs—"something that will not return ... mere words, theories, and discussions ... lighter than feathers, frightening no one." I quote here from Kundera's discussion of Nietzsche's eternal return, at the beginning of *The Unbearable Lightness of Being*. "In the sunset of dissolution," Kundera continues, "everything is illuminated by the aura of nostalgia, even the guillotine."[71]

It is *because* signifiers slide that it is possible to reconcile the eternal flux of life and death with a sense of the permanency of the self. Memory can sustain the imaginary unity of the I, not because it is anchored in a bed of authenticity, harking back to the real, but because it floats on the tide of language, behind which the real has disappeared; not because it is grounded in the surety of identity, but because it depends upon and profits from the very *différance* it so insistently denies.

WHAT'S IN A MADELEINE?

NONE OF THIS IS TO SUGGEST that the I deliberately or knowingly rewrites its biography, in the manner of the Czech censors. Such a supposition would be contrary to everything I have tried to establish so far. The weaving together of signifying chains that make past and present mirrors for one another is entirely unconscious; if it were not, it would carry no conviction, and flounder on the reefs of self-awareness. This brings us back to the vexed question of *who thinks*, which I posed earlier. For we might equally well ask—*who is the subject of memory?* Is the I who remembers, the same I whom memory constitutes as an integral self in the first place? The postulate of identity requires the answer yes, since it says that there is one and only one self. But that answer defies logic, since the self is then presupposed to the memory that constitutes it. This was the conundrum that André Breton ran into in *Nadja*, when trying to think through the dizzying proposition "I am whom I haunt." I therefore prefer the formulation I arrived at earlier, which was: *I am remembered*. Peculiar as this may sound, it conforms to the perfectly everyday experience that "I can no more summon up memories on demand than I can command myself to forget"—an experience that is every bit as mundane, yet as difficult to reconcile with Cartesian conceptions of the subject, as dreaming. But if this is the case, it follows that someone (or something) *other* must be doing the remembering—that the subject who remembers is not the same as the remembered subject that we (mis)take for the self, gazing back at us out of the mirror.

Nor do I intend to imply that our memories are simply false—notwithstanding memory's evident propensity to play fast and loose with what we normally think of as the truth. Even to pose the question of the truth of memory as an issue of authenticity, as Mirek does, is from my point of view to misunderstand what a memory is. We can never ascertain the degree of correspondence between a representation and the lost reality that it purports to represent, because the representation has already replaced the reality, and it is only this *différance* that allows us to speak of what the representation signifies at all. Even in the seemingly clear-cut case of Clementis, we may be able to establish that the photograph was doctored by comparing it with the original photograph, or with other eyewitness testimonies as to who stood on the Kinský Palace balcony beside Gottwald that snowy February day, but what we can never compare it with is *the thing itself*. The thing itself no longer exists. Here as elsewhere, truth resides entirely in the relation of terms within language, not in the relation between language and the real.

The veracity of memory—its effect of truth, as Foucault would call it[72]—is a function not of its relation with the vanished past that it re(-)presents, but wholly of its place within a signifying chain in the present of language. The airbrushing works, or not, according to how convincingly the retouched image can be reconciled with all the other representations through which the event is reconstructed—which are themselves, of course, also sliding signifiers—or put another way, with whether it can be placed in a context that gives it *meaning*. The imaginary unification of the self by and in memory takes place *entirely at the level of relations between signifiers*. Here, as elsewhere, there is no transcendental signified. It is this, I believe, that accounts for both the resilience of the self(-image) and its ultimate vulnerability. If signifiers did not defer, the self could not be continually re(-)membered and reconciled with a reality that changes all the time at all. But since they do, *différance* may always subvert the coherence of the historical narratives in which that recovered unity is articulated. Baudelaire may lead us to The Monkees, a postage stamp recall not the wartime heroism it commemorates on its face, but the trace of the Stalinist show-trials it seeks to efface.

How, then, might the subject be re-membered as an integral unified self, an identity across space and time, despite all odds? If memories are borne on signifiers, these mechanisms, too, must be linguistic.

A passage I quoted earlier from *Testaments Betrayed* lamented the paucity of the contents of our memories—"schematic and meager," was how Milan Kundera described them—by comparison with the concreteness of the real. Kundera is obviously correct in this. There will always be missing pieces in the jigsaw of what we remember, holes that are papered over, as often as not, with inaccuracies. No memory is ever complete. What remains, at best, are stray details, often recollected with extreme clarity—which is not necessarily the same thing as accuracy—that lend a patina of authenticity to a picture that, on closer inspection, proves to be mostly compounded of Baudelaire's "general colors, silhouettes, and all the arabesques of contour." (Consider here my memories of my grandparents' house in Greenford.) I believe Kundera overstates his case, however, when he claims that a diary entry (for instance) "cannot evoke a single concrete image," so that "the imagination is unable to help our memories along and reconstruct what has been forgotten."

Certainly whatever it is that the imagination reconstructs cannot be what has been forgotten, for the reasons I have given concerning the *différance* between our memories and the things (we think) we remember. But on encountering some signifier— a word, a smell, a tune on the radio—that, as we say, triggers a memory, the imagination has no difficulty whatsoever in reconstructing images of the past which are every bit as concrete as any other images that our minds may concoct for us:

> And as soon as I had recognized the taste of the piece of madeleine dipped in lime-blossom tea that my aunt used to give me ... immediately the old grey house on the street, where her bedroom was, came like a stage set to attach itself to the little wing opening on to the garden that had been built for my parents behind it (that truncated section which was all I had seen before then); and with the house the town, from morning to night and in all weathers, the Square, where they sent me before lunch, the streets where I went to run errands, the paths we took if the weather was fine. And as in that game in which the Japanese amuse themselves by filling a porcelain bowl with water and steeping in it little pieces of paper until then indistinct, which, the moment they are immersed in it, stretch and shape themselves, colour and differentiate, become flowers, houses, human figures, firm and recognizable, so now all the flowers in our garden and in M. Swann's park, and the water-lilies on the Vivonne, and the good people of the village and their little dwellings and the church and all of Combray and its surroundings, all of this which is assuming form and substance, emerged, town and gardens alike, from my cup of tea.[73]

An idyllic picture, firm and recognizable, paints itself before our eyes. It suffices only to ask, however, which flowers were in bloom, in which weathers, which errands, down which streets, which good people and when, exactly, these things happened, to recognize that this picture is a composite, akin to one of Monsieur G's creations—for assuredly what Marcel Proust recollects here never actually took place in the simultaneity in which this famous passage represents it.

What interests me most here is the sensuousness of each signifier in this nostalgic chain, beginning with the taste of the madeleine itself. So palpable are the individual elements in the picture, that we lose sight of the abstracted character of the composition as a whole. While the extent of what we remember may be pathetically meager, the manner in which we remember it is anything but schematic. A large part of the reason why memory's representation of the past convinces us is because it is underpinned by signifiers that evoke "things" extremely concrete—just like those details Monsieur G. chooses to highlight. These then create their effect of truth metonymically, by standing in for a whole synecdochically rather than mimetically replicating it. Without their presence, that whole would remain just as nebulous and abstract as Kundera says it is. Instead, they enable us almost to taste it. What alone allows these metonyms to create verisimilitude, however, is the fact that they are few in number, relative to the tumult of the once-living presents that they have come now to signify. Baudelaire observed that "multiplicity of detail" disturbs and even "paralyses" the memorizing faculty. As with Monsieur G's pictures or Ansel Adams's Rockies, the paucity of remembered detail—the radical simplification—is what makes the finished picture more *legible*. The clarity of recollection is achieved not by abstracting away from detail as such, but by zooming in on *representative* detail, the detail that *signifies*, and cropping out whatever is distracting and irrelevant, like that pesky thumb in Lange's "Migrant Mother."

Kundera is likewise surely right when he writes in *The Unbearable Lightness of Being* that we can read Nietzsche's myth of eternal return negatively, as a device that points to the fact that where there is no return, existence has no weight. "There is an infinite difference," he says, "between a Robespierre who occurs only once in history and a Robespierre who eternally returns, chopping off French heads."[74] Granted, the real itself never returns; we cannot step in the same river twice. But the signifiers that *take the place* of the real may return endlessly, if not always with the same meaning; and indeed they can do so the more readily precisely because they need *not* always have the same meaning, but obligingly defer to the nuances of time, place, and circumstance in what they bring to mind. French historians can be proud of Robespierre not (just) because, as Kundera says, the man himself will not return, but because the signifier that has replaced him may gesture to many things other than the guillotine—like Progress, the Dawn of Modernity, or the Glory of France—things on which it is pleasanter for the mind to dwell. Kundera provides an exquisitely perverse example of this kind of association himself:

> Not long ago, I caught myself experiencing a most incredible sensation. Leafing through a book on Hitler, I was touched by some of his portraits: they reminded me of my childhood. I grew up during the war; several members of my family perished in Hitler's concentration camps; but what were their deaths compared with the memories of a lost period in my life, a period that would never return?[75]

The repetition of the signifier *itself* suffices to confer a unity on memory, which does not—crucially—depend upon there being an equivalent repetition in the content of what is signified. The Slánský trial, in which Clementis forfeited his life to the Czech nation, was attended by fifteenth-century Hussite warriors, nineteenth-century national awakeners, and the much-loved illustrator of the Czech *Mother Goose*, all of whom had been bidden "Lazarus, arise!" and metaphorically co-opted for the cause of peace and progress.[76] These leading players in the socialist drama had assumed many other, no less metaphorical roles in the past. Comfortingly familiar figures, they have returned again and again throughout the years in many and varied (dis)guises, threading (together) Czech history, their presence giving it the illusion of a structure and coherence it might otherwise woefully lack. Such repetition does much to mitigate Kundera's lightness of being, without, however, always making it any the more bearable. The weight of such returns may be heavy indeed, as Vlado Clementis discovered. Had "the entire company of our great minds"[77] not been present in that Prague courtroom, the verdict might have been quite different. On the morning of his execution, December 3, 1952, the former foreign minister wrote a last letter to his wife Lída, summoning up the same distinguished company: " I am smoking a last pipe and listening. I hear you clearly singing the songs of Smetana and Dvořák. ..."[78] He could not escape the chains of the symbolic order, even on death row. I can't seem to escape all those dead sopranos and rattan canes, the ever-ready fragments of Bob Dylan songs, either.

Since, on Kundera's own premises, we can never *know* the real that is always already lost to us, but only the imagined world as constituted in language, this recurrence of the signifier—the eternal return of the never-quite-the-same, as I described it earlier—may be very much more consequential than that long-forgotten loss, which is doomed to remain forever in the realm of that whereof we cannot speak. Lacan makes the same point when he categorically states that "the value of the image as signifier has nothing whatsoever to do with its signification."[79] A portrait of Adolf Hitler may make us feel warm and cozy, an illustrator of children's books smile down on the gallows, a feared symbol of childhood punishment mutate into an object of perverse desire. This repetition is foremost among the devices through which language can create a remembered identity, not despite, but *because of* its propensity to slip and slide. It is recurring signifiers that provide the Lacanian *points de capiton* that metaphorically fix(ate) the imagined subject in a floating world, and not—as the postulate of identity leads us to assume—what they signify. The latter may morph infinitely. Every change of signification, no matter how grotesque, is concealed from the I by the reassuring repetition of the signifier itself.

Once the past has been transmuted into language, all the wiles by which language overlays meaning on the world are available for the imagination of a unitary identity that vaults spaces and collapses times, an *imago* that is not bound, as André Breton realized, by any real time or place in which the subject has actually lived. This applies equally to individuals and what Benedict Anderson has described as "imagined communities," like "nations."[80] For the *temps perdu* of the real, which we live in but can never know, is substituted the misplaced concreteness that is confected for us by words. "It is the world of words," Lacan says, "that creates the world of things—the things originally confused in the hic et nunc of the all in the process of coming-into-being—by giving its concrete being to their essence, and its ubiquity to what has always been."[81] And language has no trouble, it seems, in conjuring up in memory a more than passably concrete facsimile of identity—a *whole other self,* we could say.

This perspective clarifies other well-known tricks of memory— its ability, for instance, to mix up times, places, and events, to convince us that we perfectly recall things that we never experienced, to feel nostalgia for what we never left behind, weaving them all together into one seamless recollection of a coherent self making its solitary way through the world—the stuff of which autobiographies are made. Because memory floats on the wings of signifiers, it makes no distinction between a "genuine" experience, something one has been told, something one has read, or something one imagined in the first place. It is a planar space in which all things are equalized, flat as the two dimensions of the paper upon whose surface Monsieur G. resurrected his phantoms, while giving them all the perspectival illusion of depth. All these things may be remembered equally concretely, because their concreteness has nothing to do with their reality, but is established by and within language alone.

Coleridge's short poem "The Homeric Hexameter Described and Exemplified" says it all:

> *Strongly it bears us along in swelling and limitless billows,*
> *Nothing before and nothing behind but the sky and the ocean.*[82]

FOOTFALLS IN THE MEMORY

THE COIN OF MEMORY is the common currency of the language we all speak, which is also the language in which we can alone be spoken (of). Every memory thus partakes in and attaches its subject to the symbolic order. It is here (and only here), I think, that we can give some substance to the otherwise misleading notion of a collective memory—misleading, because only living individuals can remember—and even, perhaps, cautiously speak of a collective unconscious. Memory is always collective, in the sense that it is made up of nothing but the common stock of signifiers. But it is also always individual, because a language always presupposes a speaker: "only a subject can understand a meaning; conversely, every phenomenon of meaning implies a subject."[83] The signifiers that comprise my memories carry the entire weight of my personal history—it is certainly to be found nowhere else—and yet they also always remain the speech of what is irreducibly *other,* bearing all its traces too. To insist on this rootedness in the Other that is language, is to take nothing away from our humanity. It *is* our humanity. Which was, of course, Emile Durkheim's response to those who dreamed that they could ever be free of society, and still remain men. As Lacan puts it, "man speaks, then, but it is because the symbol has made him man."[84]

What Durkheim calls society is the supreme extraction of the eternal from the ephemeral, the ultimate beautifying lie. Insofar as we are constituted as subjects in language, we do indeed partake of the immortal and infinite, for language transcends the finite and mortal confines of (the) human being. Language once and for all removes us, or at least, that part of ourselves we can ever *know* as our selves, from the transience of the real. We are born again in *différance,* immortalized as denizens of the symbolic order, which everywhere exceeds us. There is nothing mystical about the doctrine of the soul; it grasps exactly who we are, not as corporeal beings destined to return to the dust whence we came, nor as the self-contained Cartesian egos we like to think we are, but as subjects of language. Long before poststructuralist theorists challenged the overweening hubris of the *cogito,* religions had equally radically decentered the subject. "In the beginning was the word, and the word was with God, and the word was God," begins the Gospel of St. John. The only problem is that like Humpty Dumpty, we sometimes confuse being the subjects of language with being its masters.[85]

We cannot, of course, simply dispense with our fictions of identity, whether individual or social. To believe that we could, would fly in the face of everything I have tried to argue here regarding the nature of the subject and the limits to agency. I have come to believe, nonetheless, that those moments (and we all have them) when what we experience as the self is suddenly shown up for the counterfeit it is, moments like Camus' lawyer encountered when he heard that laugh on the Pont des Arts, or Kundera's hitch-hiker suffered when her fun turned sour in that hotel room, have much to be said for them. This was the core of André Breton's argument in *Communicating Vessels,* which "tried nothing better than to cast a *conducting wire* between the far too distant worlds of waking and sleep, exterior and interior reality, reason and madness."[86] Social theorists could learn a lot from the surrealists. That laugh, as Camus was at pains to point out, had nothing mysterious about it. It was a good laugh, a hearty laugh, almost a friendly laugh. It was a laugh that "re-established the proper proportions." What was out of kilter, the whole novella invites us to infer, was rather the narrator's own *imago*— what he imagined, lighting up that loaded cigarette of quiet satisfaction, to be his identity, his complete(d) self.

Since this self, as a representation, cannot be derailed by any direct comparison with the real, its complacency may be jarred only by something that punctures the flow of the discourse in which its imagined identity is endlessly reiterated, rehearsed, performed[87]—a slip of the tongue, a double entendre, a disturbing dream, or, as in this case, a rude and apparently meaningless interruption. In using the word *puncture* here, I have in mind that *punctum* of which Roland Barthes speaks in *Camera Lucida,* when he discusses *studium* and *punctum* as elements of a photograph. The *studium* may be summarized as that which makes an image meaningful within the preoccupations of a particular time and place: "It is by *studium* that I am interested in so many photographs ... for it is culturally ... that I participate in the figures, the faces, the gestures, the settings, the actions."[88] *Studium* is what makes, for example, Edward Weston's pictures so immediately *intelligible*—at least to a modern viewer.

Not so with *punctum,* which is altogether more Proustian,[89] depending as it does on the absolute objectivity of pure chance:[90]

The second element will break (or punctuate) the *studium.* This time it is not I who seek it out (as I invest the field of the *studium* with my sovereign consciousness), it is this element which rises from the scene, shoots out of it like an arrow, and pierces me. A Latin word exists to designate this wound, this prick, this mark made by a pointed instrument: the word suits me all the better in that it also refers to the notion of punctuation, and because the photographs I am speaking of are in effect punctuated, sometimes even speckled with these sensitive points; precisely, these marks, these wounds, are so many points. This second element which will disturb the *studium* I shall therefore call *punctum*; for *punctum* is also: sting, cut, little hole—and also a cast of the dice. A photographer's *punctum* is that accident which pricks me (but also bruises me, is poignant to me).[91]

A *punctum* is a chance detail that for whatever reason (and the reason may not always be clear) stands out from its surrounding (con)text, irritating its smoothness, confounding its easy legibility—a trace, the footprint of an absence. The *punctum* is Freud's symptom, Breton's found object. Like those dead sopranos and rattan canes—or the paper knife, with ivy leaves stippled on the handle, on which was written the word **Bapaume.**

Later in the book, Barthes applies the same term to the freezing of an instant of time in an image that takes place in *any* photograph, and which is always, he says, an intimation of a death to come, because what the photographic lens captures has always already *passed away.* "This new *punctum*, which is no longer of form but of intensity," he writes, "is Time, the lacerating emphasis of the *noeme* (*'that-has-been'*) of pure representation."[92] Would it be stretching Barthes' argument too far here to suggest that the errant thumb Dorothea Lange cropped out of "Migrant Mother" might have turned out to be the *punctum* of that photograph—the point where it could have slipped from being a conventional, if powerful, iconic representation of poverty to a mortal portrait of Florence Thompson, the blemish that might have saved it from becoming kitsch? Might it also be that this determined reduction of the scene to the culturally intelligible average, the subordination of *punctum* to *studium*, lies at the root of what I so dislike in so-called documentary photography—the same difficulty as I have with "empirical" sociology, which sees in a picture of Hitler only an icon of evil, and cannot begin to elucidate the mechanisms by which distant memories of the illustrations in a book of nursery rhymes might have helped hang a one-time Czechoslovak foreign minister? Maybe: but this is not the main reason I cite Barthes here.

If, as I have argued, the (remembered) self is an *imago*, an image, then Barthes' remarks may appropriately be applied to it in both senses of the term *punctum*. The laugh on the Pont des Arts punctuates the *studium*, the discursive register in which that self is routinely made culturally intelligible to itself and others; it is the stray detail that does not fit, the signifier on the loose, which disturbs that ready (or should we perhaps say, self-evident) legibility. It pricks, it stings, it cuts, it wounds, it bruises—be it ever so trivial. And in so doing, it opens up a gap—the gap Camus' lawyer apprehended later that night when he gazed into the mirror of what would normally be the beautifying lie, and for the first time saw the smile there not as his own, but as that of his reflection. This is the gap through which time, and the intimation of death, floods in, because what was imagined to be the self has now been recognized as an *imago*, as *other*—because the identity of the I who is present with the remembered I *that-has-been* has been fractured. The timelessness that André Breton so perceptively recognized in *Nadja* as essential to the mainte-nance of his self-image, that image he haunts, is temporarily lost. And through this momentary breach in the defenses of the ego we can glimpse, if not Lacan's (or Kundera's) ineffable real, then at least the shifting sands of signification, which we fondly imag-ine to be solid rock, on which those fortifications were so pains-takingly built. Beyond the *imago* we catch sight of the unadorned subject, who is both a good deal more and very much less than the imagined I, the recollected self, that we are so used to admir-ing in the mirror—the subject who is never and can never be complete. Rimbaud grasped the truth: *j'est un autre.*[93]

None of us are in the end obliged to accept the fantasy dis-tilled out of nature, the beautifying lie, even if it makes our lives prettier, more harmonious, or more intelligible, like the undeni-ably beautiful images produced by Ansel Adams or Baudelaire's Monsieur G. Scholars and intellectuals are perhaps particularly susceptible to such blandishments. We like the world to make sense. I do not believe, however, that beauty is truth, truth beauty—much as, when I was very young, I loved the romantic poetry of John Keats.[94] In the words of André Breton in *Nad-ja*—a novel in which the author plays a less than heroic part, but emerges, for me, with enormous credibility as a human being—"I prefer, once again, walking by night to believing myself a man who walks by daylight."[95]

NOTES

1. Jacques Lacan, *Écrits: A Selection,* translated by Alan Sheridan, London and New York: Routledge, 2001, p. 182.

2. George Seferis, "Mythical Story," in Edward Keeley and Philip Sherrard (eds.), *Four Greek Poets,* Harmondsworth: Penguin, 1966, p. 48.

3. See Roland Barthes, "The Death of the Author," in *Image, Music, Text,* New York: Hill and Wang, 1977, p. 145.

4. Ludwig Wittgenstein, *Tractatus Logico-Philosophicus,* London: Routledge and Kegan Paul, 1971, p. 115; original emphasis.

5. Jacques Lacan, "The Mirror-Stage as Formative of the Function of the *I,*" in *Écrits,* pp. 1–8.

6. Jacques Derrida, *Monolingualism of the Other, or The Prosthesis of Origin,* Stanford: Stanford University Press, 1998, p. 1.

7. Lacan, *Écrits,* p. 94.

8. Emile Durkheim, "The Dualism of Human Nature and Its Social Conditions," in R. N. Bellah (ed.), *Emile Durkheim on Morality and Society,* Chicago: Chicago University Press, 1973, p. 150.

9. *Ibid.,* pp. 150–151.

10. *Ibid.,* p. 162.

11. Emile Durkheim, "The Determination of Moral Facts," in *Sociology and Philosophy,* New York: Free Press, 1974, p. 57.

12. Emile Durkheim, "Replies to Objections," in *Sociology and Philosophy,* p. 73.

13. Jacques Derrida, *Positions,* translated by Alan Bass, Chicago: University of Chicago Press, 1982, pp. 19–20.

14. Don DeLillo, *The Body Artist,* New York: Simon and Schuster, 2001, p. 84.

15. See Derrida, *Positions,* pp. 24–29, for a succinct summary. The notion is explained more fully in "Différance," in Jacques Derrida, *Margins of Philosophy,* translated by Alan Bass, Chicago: Chicago University Press, 1986, pp. 1–29.

16. Lacan, *Écrits,* pp. 169–70.

17. Derrida, *Positions,* p. 26.

18. See for instance "The Subject and Power," in James D. Faubion (ed.), *Michel Foucault: Power,* New York: New Press, 2000, pp. 326–348. The key point, in the present context, is that: "There are two meanings of the word 'subject': subject to someone else by control and dependence, and tied to his own identity by a conscience or self-knowledge. Both meanings suggest a form of power that subjugates and makes subject to" (p. 331).

19. "Our language and our social relations are just two different sides of the same coin. To give an account of the meaning of a word is to describe how it is used; and to describe how it is used is to describe the social intercourse into which it enters." Peter Winch, *The Idea of a Social Science and Its relation to Philosophy*, London: Routledge and Kegan Paul, 1963, p. 123.

20. Durkheim, "Determination of Moral Facts," p. 48.

21. Derrida, *Positions*, pp. 28–29.

22. Lacan, *Écrits*, pp. 22, 61.

23. I should like to stress here that the arguments developed throughout this essay apply as much to collective as to individual identities. See my book *The Coasts of Bohemia: A Czech History*, Princeton: Princeton University Press, 1998. While less explicitly theoretical than this essay, this book was an exploration of identity in relation to memory in the case of a national history. It provides an example of how the "poststructuralist" perspective on identity advocated here might affect both historical and sociological scholarship, by shifting the focus of empirical inquiry to *how* an identity is imagined into being (and memories continually re-membered as an essential part of that process), rather than taking it as an unproblematic framework within which a history is retrospectively written.

24. "The Painter of Modern Life," in Charles Baudelaire, *My Heart Laid Bare and Other Prose Writings*, London: Soho Book Company, 1986, p. 37.

25. *Ibid.*

26. I am gesturing here to the opening pages of Clifford Geertz, *After the Fact: Two Countries, Four Decades, One Anthropologist*, Cambridge: Harvard University Press, 1996; and also to Maurice Blanchot's essay "After the Fact," in *The Station Hill Blanchot Reader: Fiction and Literary Essays*, edited by George Quasha, Barrytown: Station Hill, 1999, pp. 487–496.

27. Baudelaire, "The Painter of Modern Life," p. 31.

28. *Ibid.*, pp. 31–32.

29. *Ibid.*, pp. 32, 34, 33.

30. *Ibid.*, p. 35.

31. *Ibid.*, p. 36.

32. *Ibid.*, pp. 41–44.

33. Karl Marx and Friedrich Engels, *The Holy Family*, in *Collected Works*, Vol. 4, London: Lawrence and Wishart, 1995, pp. 57–60.

34. Lange's "Migrant Mother" is discussed in detail, and a number of variants of the picture reproduced, in Hans-Michael Koetzle,

Photo Icons: The Story Behind the Pictures, Vol. 2, Köln: Taschen, 2002, pp. 28–37. See also the introduction to Mark Durden, *Dorothea Lange,* London and New York: Phaidon, 2001.

35. Edward Weston, "Seeing Photographically," in Alan Trachtenberg (ed.), *Classic Essays on Photography,* New Haven: Leete's Island Books, p. 174.

36. Siegfried Kracauer, "Photography," in Trachtenberg, *Classic Essays on Photography,* p. 251.

37. In James Agee, *Let Us Now Praise Famous Men,* Boston: Houghton Mifflin, 2000.

38. These are allusions to paintings by Grant Wood and Andrew Wyeth respectively.

39. Baudelaire, "The Painter of Modern Life," p. 36; emphasis added.

40. Quoted in Susan Sontag, *On Photography,* New York: Picador, 1977, p. 184.

41. "'I think.' Nietzsche cast doubt on this assertion dictated by a grammatical convention that every verb must have a subject. Actually, said he, 'a thought comes when "it" wants to, and not when "I" want it to; so that it is falsifying the fact to say that the subject "I" is necessary to the verb "think."' A thought comes to the philosopher 'from outside, from above or below, like events or thunderbolts heading for him.'" Milan Kundera, *Testaments Betrayed,* New York: HarperCollins, 1995, p. 149.

42. Lacan, *Écrits,* p. 183.

43. Or maybe, of course, I am. My doubts regarding at least common interpretations of Freud relate to the usual notion of the unconscious as "some obscure will regarded as primordial ... something pre-conscious," to which (according to Lacan's interpretation, anyway) "what Freud opposes is the revelation that at the level of the unconscious there is something at all points homologous with what occurs at the level of the subject—this thing speaks and functions in a way quite as elaborate as at the level of the conscious, which thus loses what seemed to be its privilege." Jacques Lacan, *The Four Fundamental Concepts of Psychoanalysis,* translated by Alan Sheridan, edited by Jacques-Alain Miller, New York: Norton, 1998, p. 24. Derrida likewise repudiates any "metaphysical" conception of the unconscious (and with it the romantic idea that the primordially "authentic" self is to be located there): "A certain alterity—to which Freud gives the metaphysical name of the unconscious—is definitively exempt from every process of presentation by means of which

we would call upon it to show itself in person. In this context, and in this guise, the unconscious is not, as we know, a hidden, virtual, or potential self-presence. It differs from, and defers, itself; which doubtless means that it is woven of differences, and also that it sends out delegates, representatives, proxies; but without any chance that the giver of proxies might 'exist,' might be present, be 'itself' somewhere, and with even less of a chance that it might become conscious. In this sense, contrary to the terms of an old debate full of the metaphysical investments that it has always assumed, the 'unconscious' is no more a 'thing' than it is any other thing, it is no more a thing than it is a virtual or masked consciousness" (Derrida, *Margins of Philosophy*, pp. 20–21). Exactly.

44. I am alluding to André Breton, *Anthology of Black Humor*, translated by Mark Polizzotti, San Francisco: City Lights, 1997.

45. Derrida, *Positions*, pp. 40–41.

46. André Breton, *Nadja*, translated by Richard Howard, New York: Grove Press, 1960, p. 11.

47. *Ibid.*

48. My translation of Freud's German is literal here. Lacan renders it as "I must come to the place where that was." *Écrits*, p. 189.

49. Breton, *Nadja*, p. 12.

50. Baudelaire, "The Painter of Modern Life," pp. 33–34.

51. Albert Camus, *The Fall*, translated by Justin O'Brien, New York: Vintage, 1991, pp. 38–40.

52. Pierre Nora et al., *Realms of Memory: The Construction of the French Past*, New York: Columbia University Press, 1996, pp. 1–20; see especially Nora's General Introduction.

53. Milan Kundera, *The Book of Laughter and Forgetting*, translated by Michael Henry Heim, London: Penguin, 1986, p. 3.

54. Ivan Klíma, *Love and Garbage*, translated by Ewald Osers, New York: Vintage, 1993, p. 45.

55. George Orwell, *Nineteen Eighty-Four*, in *The Penguin Complete Novels of George Orwell*, London: Penguin, 1983, pp. 764–767. "'Who controls the past,' ran the Party slogan, 'controls the future: who controls the present controls the past'" (p. 762). The "rectification" of back-copies of newspapers (and all other documents) is discussed on pp. 764–767, at the start of chapter 4 of the novel. Once they had been rewritten, the originals were stuffed down what were nicknamed "memory holes," where they were pneumatically sped to a furnace. Orwell comments: "Day by day and almost minute by minute the past was brought up to date. ...

All history was a palimpsest, scraped clean and reinscribed exactly as often as was necessary."

56. See Jean Baudrillard, *Symbolic Exchange and Death,* translated by Iain H. Grant, London: Sage, 1993.

57. Milan Kundera, *The Art of the Novel,* translated by Linda Asher, New York: Grove Press, 1988, p. 130.

58. *Ibid.,* p. 130.

59. Kundera, *Testaments Betrayed,* pp. 128–129.

60. Maurice Blanchot, "Two Versions of the Imaginary," in *The Station Hill Blanchot Reader,* p. 419.

61. Milan Kundera, "The Hitchhiking Game," in *Laughable Loves,* translated by Suzanne Rappaport, New York: HarperCollins, 1999, pp. 105–106.

62. Kundera, *Art of the Novel,* p. 28.

63. *Ibid.,* p. 135.

64. See, for example, his essay "A Kidnapped West or Culture Bows Out," in *Granta,* no. 11, 1984, pp. 93–122.

65. Zdeněk Nejedlý, preface to the exhibition catalog *Celostátní výstava archivních dokumentu: od hrdinně minulosti k vítěvství socialismu,* Prague: Ministerstvo vnitra, 1958, p. 7.

66. See my *Coasts of Bohemia.*

67. Kundera elaborates on this in his interview with Christian Salmon, which forms Part 2 of *The Art of the Novel.*

68. It may perhaps be that modernity speeds up this turnover, and to that degree we might wish to historicize this remark. See, for example, Marshall Berman, *All That Is Solid Melts into Air: The Experience of Modernity,* New York: Simon and Schuster, 1982— though we should also be wary, here as elsewhere, of taking modernity at face-value, read through its own characteristic grand narratives.

69. Lacan, *Écrits,* p. 57.

70. Julian Barnes, *England, England,* London: Jonathan Cape, 1998, p. 3.

71. Milan Kundera, *The Unbearable Lightness of Being,* translated by Michael Henry Heim, New York: HarperCollins, pp. 3–4.

72. See Michel Foucault, *The Order of Things: An Archaeology of the Human Sciences,* New York: Vintage, 1994.

73. Marcel Proust, *The Way by Swann's* [Volume 1 of *In Search of Lost Time*], translated by Lydia Davis, London: Allen Lane, 2002, p. 50.

74. Kundera, *Unbearable Lightness of Being,* p. 4.

75. *Ibid.*

76. During the period that followed the communist takeover in Czechoslovakia in 1948, a determined effort was made to resuscitate the discourse and heroes of the nineteenth-century "national revival" to legitimate the new regime. I discuss this at length in chapter 7 of *The Coasts of Bohemia*. See also my paper "A Quintessential Czechness," *Common Knowledge*, vol. 7, no. 2, 1998, pp. 136–164.

77. As the artist Max Švabinský described the occupants of Vyšehrad cemetery in Prague, in which leading Czech artists, writers, and composers had been buried since the mid-nineteenth century, at the funeral of Alfons Mucha on July 19, 1939. See *The Coasts of Bohemia*, pp. 19–21.

78. Quoted (and original Czech source given) in *The Coasts of Bohemia*, p. 239. Smetana and Dvořák are quintessentially *Czech* composers.

79. Lacan, *Écrits*, p. 176. Earlier he refers to "the illusion that the signifier answers to the function of representing the signified, or better, that the signifier has to answer for its existence in the name of any signification whatsoever" (p. 166).

80. Benedict Anderson, *Imagined Communities: Reflections on the Origins and Spread of Nationalism*, rev. ed., London: Verso, 1991.

81. Lacan, *Écrits*, p. 72.

82. Samuel Taylor Coleridge, "The Homeric Hexameter Described and Exemplified," in *Coleridge: Poems and Prose* (ed.), Kathleen Raine, London: Penguin, 1957, p. 90.

83. Lacan, *Écrits*, p. 11.

84. *Ibid.*, p. 72.

85. See Lewis Carroll, *Alice's Adventures in Wonderland and Through the Looking Glass*, New York: Knopf, 1993, pp. 254–255.

86. André Breton, *Communicating Vessels*, translated by Mary Ann Caws and Geoffrey T. Harris, Lincoln: University of Nebraska Press, 1990, p. 86.

87. See Judith P. Butler, *Gender Trouble*, New York: Routledge, 1990.

88. Roland Barthes, *Camera Lucida*, translated by Richard Howard, New York: Hill and Wang, 2000, p. 26.

89. See Proust, *The Way by Swann's*, p. 47. He writes: "It is the same with our past. It is a waste of effort for us to try to summon it, all the exertions of our intelligence are useless. The past is hidden outside the realm of our intelligence and beyond its reach, in some

material object (in the sensation which this material object would give us) which we do not suspect. It depends on chance whether we encounter this object before we die, or do not encounter it." See also Walter Benjamin, "Surrealism: The Last Snapshot of the European Intelligentsia," on memory, what may be incarnated in material objects, and what he considers to be surrealism's discoveries in this field (in *Walter Benjamin: Selected Writings, Volume 2, 1927–1934*, translated by Rodney Livingstone et al., edited by Michael W. Jennings, Howard Eiland, and Gary Smith, Cambridge, Mass: The Belknap Press of Harvard University Press, 1999).

90. The notion of *hazard objectif* originated with Breton and the surrealists. Compare Gerhard Richter, "Interview with Benjamin H. D. Buchlow, 1986," in *The Daily Practice of Painting: Writings 1962–1993*, translated by David Britt, London: Thames and Hudson, 1995, p. 159.

91. Barthes, *Camera Lucida*, pp. 26–27.

92. *Ibid.*, pp. 95–96.

93. See Lacan, *Écrits*, p. 26.

94. "'Beauty is truth, truth beauty'—that is all / Ye know on earth, and all ye need to know." John Keats, "Ode on a Grecian Urn," in Denys Kilham Roberts (ed.), *The Centuries' Poetry, Volume 3, Pope to Keats*, Harmondsworth: Penguin, 1950.

95. Breton, *Nadja*, p. 60.

INDEX

Index

PERMISSIONS

ABOUT THE AUTHOR

Derek Sayer was born in London, England, in 1950, educated at the Universities of Essex and Durham, and moved to Canada in 1986. He currently holds the Canada Research Chair in Social Theory and Cultural Studies at the University of Alberta. He is the author of ten books, including *The Coasts of Bohemia: A Czech History* (Princeton University Press 1998), *Capitalism and Modernity* (Routledge 1991), and *The Great Arch* (with Philip Corrigan, Blackwell 1985).